Praise for ....

"Whether leading or following, you need to read *Initiative*. I have long yearned for such a book—the most clear and persuasive on personal development and leadership I've found in 60 years of adulthood. Spodek's focus on initiative and reflection matches what I found effective serving in and leading organizations from a few people to over 15,000 Marines and Sailors. He illustrates key ideas with meaningful examples and helpful practical exercises. It's lucid, succinct, easy to read, and deeply profound. It has earned a prominent place in my library."

LIEUTENANT GENERAL PAUL K. VAN RIPER U.S. Marine Corps (Retired)

"Many congratulations to Josh Spodek for *Initiative*! I loved his comparison of *Shark Tank* to the dog show. The common 'wisdom' of expecting passion to automatically lead to action only works if you're amazingly lucky. *Initiative* gives you a powerful tool kit to explore your interests and passions and create what makes you excited to work—how to make your own luck. No more Monday morning blues. If you work through the exercises here, you'll stop saying 'somebody should fix that' and become the one who does, to the world's benefit, and especially your own."

ALAN INY global leader, creativity and scenarios, Boston Consulting Group and coauthor of *Thinking in New Boxes: A New Paradigm for Business Creativity*

"Joshua Spodek restores the humanity, soul, and passion to the entrepreneurial spirit that built our nation. With simple steps and diverse stories, *Initiative* walks you through finding your passion and bringing it to life with confidence."

FRANCES HESSELBEIN Presidential Medal of Freedom honoree and president and CEO of the Frances Hesselbein Leadership Institute

"The disease is helplessness and inaction, and Joshua Spodek has the cure: *Initiative*. By taking initiative, we can connect with our passions and with people who can nurture those passions into actionable ideas that make money, create happiness, or maybe even change the world. Spodek starts off with some hard truths about today's business environment, then follows up with Method Initiative, a series of exercises that will help you identify your interests and create those connections that lead to success."

DANIEL H. PINK author of *When* and *Drive*

"If you've ever wanted to start a project but weren't sure how, *Initiative* is the missing piece. With effective, step-by-step exercises and engaging real-life stories, this book will show you how to become someone who can start projects you love from scratch."

DORIE CLARK professor at Duke University's Fuqua School of Business and author of *Entrepreneurial You* and *Stand Out*

"Why do people with the *most* education often feel they have the *fewest* options? Spodek offers a brilliant critique of the ways our education system kills students' initiative. In a step-by-step fashion, he goes on to show you how to regain yours. A 'remedial class' everyone should take!"

TONY WAGNER EdD, bestselling author of *The Global Achievement Gap* and *Creating Innovators* and senior research fellow, Learning Policy Institute

"Joshua found what was missing from entrepreneurship! *Initiative* shows why most entrepreneurial resources are counterproductive for people outside Silicon Valley. Then it shows *actionable* steps based on real-life results, illustrated with real-life stories from Joshua's decade-plus of research, teaching, and coaching. You will discover skills, confidence, and passions you always knew you had."

MARSHALL GOLDSMITH Thinkers50 #1 in leadership and world's #1 executive coach

"Initiative, action, and passion comprise one of the most important and overlooked virtuous circles in life. This book is your guide to implementing an empowering, world-changing feedback loop no matter what your age, interests, or professional calling."

JONAS KOFFLER *New York Times*–bestselling author of *Hustle*

"Joshua shows that not only are many of our fundamental entrepreneurship practices wrong and misguided, they can be downright counterproductive. What works for TV shows or Silicon Valley actually *inhibit* the rest of us from acting on passions that can get us promoted, hired, and funded. *Initiative*'s surprisingly simple steps and real-life profiles of people who started from nothing show you how to bring them to life."

DAVID BURKUS bestselling author, speaker, and professor of leadership at Oral Roberts University

"Entrepreneurship is my jam! It's disappointing how TV shows, movies, and universities discourage people from following their FIRE. *Initiative* cuts through the hype and myth. Joshua Spodek *gets it* and this book is proof. *Initiative* shows you what works and how people are implementing change in the world today."

JOHN LEE DUMAS founder and host of the "Best of iTunes" *Entrepreneurs on Fire* podcast

"We endure far more than we have to at work, and yet there we sit, stuck. What holds us back from yanking ourselves out of our malaise? Joshua Spodek knows, and knows what to do about it. He unlocks the ultimate power—initiative—through insight and powerful exercises to give you the experiences, skills, and beliefs needed to get things going, no matter what you're trying to accomplish. Take the initiative to buy this book—you won't regret it."

SCOTT MAUTZ popular keynote speaker and author of *Find the Fire* and *Make It Matter*

"Another thought-provoking, life-changing book from Joshua Spodek. For anyone who wants to take the initiative to launch a business, get a new job, or change the world—this book is for you."

KEVIN KRUSE CEO of LEADX and author of *Great Leaders Have No Rules*

"I've seen many people create greatness in their lives and work. *Initiative* teaches you how, *by doing*. Its real-life stories of people of diverse backgrounds and interests make the exercises and principles accessible to diverse readers. Its vivid imagery makes challenging concepts simple to understand and visualize."

TOM ZIGLAR CEO of Ziglar, Inc. and proud son of Zig Ziglar

INITIATIVE

ISBN 978-1-7330399-0-1 (paperback)
ISBN 978-1-7330399-1-8 (ebook)

Greenwich Lane Books
joshuaspodek.com

Produced by Page Two
www.pagetwo.com
Cover design by Peter Cocking
Interior design by Setareh Ashrafologhalai

joshuaspodek.com
spodekacademy.com

JOSHUA SPODEK

INITIATIVE

*A Proven Method to Bring Your
Passions to Life (and Work)*

EVEN (ESPECIALLY) IF YOU DON'T KNOW YOURS YET

Greenwich Lane
BOOKS

CONTENTS

PREFACE

RAFAEL

Rafael came to me for help. He couldn't stand his managers at the media firm where he worked. He had an MBA and an undergraduate degree from top schools and had worked hard to reach his position. He earned plenty of money and performed well. He wanted to participate in strategic decisions. The firm was small, but they never accepted his proposals.

He said, "Josh, I can't work for other people anymore. I have to start a company. You've started companies. Please help me start one." He didn't have an idea or team. He didn't know what company he would start. He wanted something different.

We started working together. I coached Rafael through a simple program of exercises to help him find direction and reach his goals. A few months later, instead of having started a new venture, he was working happily at the same firm on a project that his managers valued and gave him ownership over.

They gave him responsibility for his project's success or failure, which before might have caused him anxiety, but they also gave him the autonomy and resources to make success happen, which turned anxiety to enthusiasm, even excitement. He also worked fewer hours for the same pay. He was happier, more productive, and enjoyed his time and relationships at work.

He took no time off or formal classes. He only did those few exercises with me. His managers didn't change. He didn't suddenly get another degree. He didn't magically become reborn with new skills or learn them from watching *Shark Tank*.

How did he create this result?

He created his project, involving his managers in the process, so they happily gave him ownership. He helped them enough that they helped him back.

Looking back, he saw that he wanted responsibility and ownership—not the low-level, non-operational parts of starting a company, like finding office space and registering with the state. He felt he needed to act dramatically because he only knew two options: to stay or leave. He didn't see the option to take initiative to create an outcome he wanted.

What changed?

Rafael developed the social and emotional skills, experiences, and beliefs to solve a problem that he cared about, helping others enough that they rewarded him for it. He created a supportive community. That is, he took initiative to find a problem worth solving, figure out tentative solutions, work with the relevant people to refine the solution, and show people with resources how he would do it.

What he did wasn't hard. He enjoyed it more than the work on his job description. He had just never taken initiative like that before. In fact, his formal education had prepared him for the opposite—to comply and follow.

Involving the decision-makers in the process led them to trust him and feel a vested interest in his success. He put the resources the project needed in the plan his managers helped him create, so that marshaling those resources became part of the project. He didn't need impossible-to-get connections, funding, or any other resource to start. He didn't need to be born with special genes or a gift to sell.

Taking initiative uncovered passion that he'd always had but didn't sense. He could have acted earlier, but thought he had to do everything himself. He thought he needed answers for *everything* before presenting *anything*. He didn't see that he had access to people, including his managers, who could have provided what resources he needed.

He took initiative in business, but Rafael could have applied the same skills with his family, friends, community, or in any part of his life. In fact, he later did.

What Happened to Taking Initiative?

Rafael's starting situation is common. Sadly, his transformation is rare, though as accessible to anyone as it was to him. A kitchen full of ingredients and utensils won't help you make dinner if you don't know how to cook. On the contrary, knowing you could do something in theory but can't in practice makes you feel frustrated, as Rafael did. You need to build skills, by starting with a few simple recipes. It helps if someone can walk you through your first experiences.

People everywhere in all walks of life feel stuck in their work, hobbies, and social lives. Like Rafael, they see the alternatives as so big and challenging that they're not worth trying until their situation has become unbearable. So they endure just bearable limits.

If a few months of exercises, without time off or formal classes, was all Rafael needed to transform his work, why didn't he know how to take initiative? Why hadn't his education prepared him? Why did he default to the overkill of starting a new company?

Doesn't our culture celebrate entrepreneurship in top-rated television shows, magazines, movies, and biographies? Bookstores fill sections with entrepreneurship books. Why did none of these abundant resources help him? Why, amid plenty, did Rafael feel stranded?

Why do so many like him feel so stranded? Aren't entrepreneurship and initiative more active than ever?

Not according to the data. The *New York Times* reported[1] that "the share of younger companies—less than one year old—in the United States has declined by almost half over the last generation," lamenting, "the startup decline might defy expectations in the age of Uber and *Shark Tank*. But however counterintuitive, the trend is backed by multiple data sources and numerous economic studies."

The article continued, "In 1980, according to the Census Bureau data, roughly one in eight companies had been founded in the past year; by 2015, that ratio had fallen to fewer than one in 12. The downward trend cuts across regions and industries and, at least since 2000, includes even the beating heart of American entrepreneurship, high tech."

The effect is global. The *New York Times* has also reported[2] that "the economy's ability to generate and support new businesses— agents of creative destruction that bring new products and methods into the marketplace—appears to be faltering across the world. In the United States, the rate of company formation is half what it was four decades ago. And it is slowing in many industrialized countries."

What if Uber and *Shark Tank* are *exacerbating* entrepreneurship's decline? And how did the entrepreneurial spirit at the foundation of capitalism become a media spectacle anyway?

How did solving problems and starting projects become so institutionalized? What happened to plain old *initiative*? When the threshold to launch becomes so high, what falls through the cracks? Why does our society fail so many people who could take initiative?

The neglected problems and people are the tip of the iceberg. Greater is the helplessness and dependence our culture creates, depriving us of the skill to sense opportunities and act on them. We've created the myth that you need passion to start, or, conversely, that only by doing something big will passion emerge. What held Rafael back wasn't a lack of opportunity but of experience, skill, and the belief to see and act on opportunities already there. Beginners see black and white—take what you get or throw it all away and start from scratch. Masters see nuance and subtle indications of unsolved problems that others will reward them for solving.

What works—what develops passion and gets the job done—is easier, more fun, and more rewarding.

Part One of this book is the story of what's holding you—and much of the population—back. Part Two is a set of exercises to develop the skills, experiences, and beliefs needed to take initiative, all of which are applicable to any part of your life—what I call *Method Initiative*. Throughout this book are profiles and stories of people who practiced the exercises in Part Two and learned to take initiative. They succeeded in every way they care about—their projects, their joy of discovering and acting on their passions, and helping their communities. Doing the exercises will teach you how to achieve in your life what they did in theirs.

The exercises are simple, straightforward, and not a scattered assortment. They are a comprehensive progression designed, tested, and refined by hundreds of students and clients. They are based on a style of learning practiced in other fields, around the world, for centuries, but mostly neglected in teaching initiative or entrepreneurship, even (especially) at top universities and business schools.

They cover what successful entrepreneurs and initiators do, but existing literature, media, TED talks, and other resources miss. You will see the deep relationships between initiative, action, and passion, and how each contributes to and needs the others. Instead of pushing hard on one, I will show you how engaging all three in a cycle can take you from where you are to any level of mastery you want.

You will read why most entrepreneurial resources and educational programs don't help about 94 percent of us. You'll see why people who claim to help can lead you astray—for their benefit, not yours, and often to your loss.

None of the people profiled started with special advantages. Some started as gray-haired professionals. Others were in college, some in high school. Some worked with me one-on-one, others in group courses, and others through my online course. Most didn't start

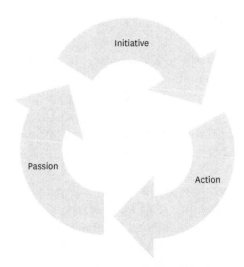

with ideas. In fact, many didn't know they'd start projects affecting actual people at all, instead anticipating a regular academic class with papers and tests. In other words, you don't need an idea, a team, or to know your passions to reach success.

You will see how entrepreneurship is a subset of initiative, and why entrepreneurship books, videos, and courses help only a small number of people. You'll see why we've institutionalized entrepreneurship into reality TV, media spectacles, and personalities, all distracting from what works.

Initiative is simpler and applies more broadly than entrepreneurship. It can mean starting a for-profit company, but also starting a non-profit, organizing your community, earning a raise, gaining responsibility, starting a new division, creating a hobby, changing your lifestyle, planning a family vacation everyone loves, or solving many problems in a way others will value you for. You might start a movement.

Rafael, as it turns out, started a company a few years later—with confidence and without coaching from me, on his own initiative and on friendly terms with the company he left, profitable from month one—that he still runs today. He's applied what he learned throughout his life, beyond business too.

Initiative for the Rest of Us

Rafael wasn't born with any special talents, nor were his results unique. You can achieve them too, and this book will show you how.

I've taught how to take initiative to students and clients of diverse backgrounds, goals, and ages. You'll meet several in later chapters. They love the results. Despite not knowing that they'd start meaningful projects, let alone specific ideas, they went on from their classwork to be featured in the *Washington Post*, the *Wall Street Journal*, *Forbes*, and *Inc.*; others have spoken at Harvard and TEDx; one was named a Dalai Lama fellow; others earned raises, promotions, new responsibilities, and job offers.

They founded ventures and non-profits; won awards and grants; improved relationships with spouses, parents, children, colleagues; got accepted to schools—even ones that had previously rejected them—and more.

They have received funding and support from Harvard, Y Combinator, former Google CEO Eric Schmidt, and Facebook founder Mark Zuckerberg. Many projects led to job offers, raises, and promotions to work on their projects without leaving where they were.

Beyond creating *one* successful project, they learned to create successful projects *in general*. They learned to work independently of institutionalized entrepreneurship. They learned to create projects based on their interests and develop relationships with valuable people who can support them, and who have a vested interest in their success.

They uncovered passions they didn't know they had and learned to act on them successfully. They faced doubts and inhibitions and learned how to replace them with confidence, independence, and an expectation of success. They learned to love their work.

These abilities change everything. People who finished the exercises say things like:

> "I would highly recommend this course to someone who is interested in the idea of starting their own venture but hasn't had

the confidence, support, or general idea of the way in which to go about it. I would also recommend this course to people who would like to meet fellow students who have diverse passions and are highly motivated to explore them."

"I am a Stern alum who concentrated in Management, and Joshua Spodek's class better taught me more applicable and meaningful management skills than any courses from the Management Department."

"10/10 would take again! I loved every second of this class, but what's cooler is that I think I may have loved the homework even more."

"It was an incredible class that inspired me in immeasurable ways. It was my first real experiential course in college and thus allowed me to feel prepared to actually use the skills I learned in the real world."

"It gave me a new sense of citizenship."

"This is an extremely hands-on practical class. What you put in, you'll get out."

"This is one of the greatest classes I have ever taken. It was engaging, thought provoking, challenging, and fun. Josh is an incredible teacher, mentor, and friend to everyone in the class who is passionate about the subject matter. If I could take this class all over again, I would."

I include these quotes knowing that they raise your expectations, which risks me overpromising. If you do the exercises as described, I expect they will overdeliver on even high expectations because you will live the results, not just read about them. You have to do the work, though.

I speak and teach from experience, not just theory. I live this way. By doing what this book teaches, I've accomplished so much that hosts introducing me can't believe it: five Ivy League degrees;

speaking at TEDx, Harvard, Princeton, West Point, Boston Consulting Group, IBM, and other globally admired firms; creating a company with an eight-digit valuation operating on four continents; writing several patents; competing in sports at national and world levels; creating big public art pieces in Manhattan and showing in museums and solo gallery shows; appearing in major media outlets in print, broadcast, and online; teaching at top universities to stellar reviews; working with Nobel laureates, Super Bowl champions, Olympic medalists, a CrossFit Games champion, a Presidential Medal of Freedom honoree, four-star generals, Victoria's Secret models, and C-suite executives at Fortune 100 companies; writing a bestseller; creating an award-winning podcast... the list goes on. All enjoyable, fun, and rewarding. All results of initiative.

Life after mastering the skills of taking initiative means identifying and activating passions you didn't know you had. It means living a deliberate life of passion with passionate people supporting and helping you because you help and support them.

ONE

WHO STOLE INITIATIVE?

question - Why did Spodex
choose to work with
many companys + foundations
instead of a main job?

comment - I like how he uses
(pos) his human problem examples
to show how he + his
methods work.

concern - I was a little
(neg) confused on how
The dog shows related
to initiare + entrepweshup

1

THE PROBLEM

The Dog Show

You know the Westminster Kennel Club dog show even if you haven't attended.

Maybe you've seen the movie *Best in Show*, which satirized events like it. The *New York Times*' description of a recent winner illustrates such dog shows: "[He] cut a striking, cloudlike figure in the ring: His powder-puff fur was painstakingly coifed, and he trotted jauntily across the floor with a step that looked almost lighter than air."

Westminster means *painstakingly coifed* purebreds *trotting jauntily*.

Over 3,000 dogs, handlers, and owners compete in Madison Square Garden for Best in Show each year at Westminster. The finale begins with the announcement of the Best in Breed winners, who run out through a chute with their handlers to do a lap before the cheering fans filling the stands.

The main competition is about to begin. Handlers and their dogs wait obediently. A judge steps to the center of the floor and congratulates them for reaching this stage.

The judge approaches each dog in turn, inspecting each by hand and eye. At the judge's command, the handlers and dogs perform. Fans alternate between hushed anticipation and excited cheers.

After enough evaluation, the judge prepares to pronounce the winners, moving to the center. Drawing out each moment, playing the crowd, the judge announces the third-place winner... the second...

Then the winner!

The crowd goes wild. The winner becomes a jauntily trotting, painstakingly coifed celebrity.

Dogs and the Rest of Us

I asked some friends to describe the Westminster dog show. They said:

"People go crazy over the spectacle even though it's weird and not for the dogs."

"It's silly, I would think I would never watch, but it draws you in."

"It's fascinating, terrifying, and engaging when it shouldn't be. I don't really care about dogs."

"I can't figure out why it's engaging, mysteriously. It's good TV though."

I grew up with a different dog experience. My family owned many dogs. I loved them all, but my favorite was Jake, a standard poodle. Here he is, next to a Westminster poodle:

My dog, Jake

A Westminster poodle

I doubt Jake would have won any competitions. I doubt they would have let him in the building. I loved him no less. As best I could tell, he loved me back. Westminster is a different world from Jake's, irrelevant to my relationship with dogs—or to anyone's that I've seen.

The technical name for Westminster is a *conformation show*—competitions for how well dogs conform to their standards. Conformation shows don't judge if a hunting dog can hunt. They judge if it *looks* like their definition of how a hunting dog should look. Their revenue comes from tickets and sponsorship. They make money *off* dogs, not *with* them.

That's not to say that dog shows aren't perfect for many people. I believe the people who run them and participate in them care about dogs as much as anyone. They're a matter of taste.

From the perspective of dog people I know, though, conformation shows seem alien, even weird. They focus on one type of relationship: obedience—from dog to handler, handler to owner, and all to the judge. The handlers don't run and play with the dogs, they trot, also jauntily. The floor is green carpet, not grass. Conformation shows lead to inbreeding, increasing some breeds' susceptibility to disease. Some are bred to where they have trouble breathing and giving birth.

If conformation shows were the only way to own a dog I suspect few would own them, which would be sad, because there are as many ways to love dogs as there are dogs and owners.

Dog Shows, Initiative, and Entrepreneurship

What does all this have to do with initiative and entrepreneurship? People who have participated in business plan competitions describe them similarly to dog shows:

"It was a distraction from customers who should decide if you succeed; a real clash of interests."

"It's a hype cycle between who can pitch the best, which may correlate with who can sell best, but, from the investor perspective, it can narrow the field."

"From the entrepreneur's standpoint, now you have to be a dancing monkey, and it motivates learning to dance more than running a business."

We've turned initiative and entrepreneurship into a dog show.

Shark Tank, business plan competitions, media hype, and various players benefit more from making a spectacle of entrepreneurship than from its successful practice, often ignoring projects outside their mold. They'd see Rafael's in-house initiative as Westminster would see Jake. Many make more money *off* entrepreneurs than *with* them. They lead startup founders and managers to compete for the judges instead of focusing on customers, employees, and operations.

I call this institution *Dog Show Entrepreneurship*—high-tech, fast-growth, investor-backed, founders-in-their-20s, companies emerging from a Silicon Valley–like environment. As with conformation shows, it's perfect for some. I suggest no malice on the part of those who promote it. I believe they care about entrepreneurship as much as anyone, at least their type of it. They're just looking after their interests, which sometimes conflict with those of entrepreneurs and initiators.

From the perspective of successful initiators and entrepreneurs outside Dog Show Entrepreneurship, it looks alien, even weird. It focuses on obedience to judges whose interests often conflict with the long-term success of the startup and its stakeholders. It distracts entrepreneurs' attention from their customers, employees, and operations. Instead of building enduring relationships, they create elevator pitches. They painstakingly coif and trot jauntily.

Despite Dog Show Entrepreneurship appearances, there are as many ways to start a project as there are initiators and problems to solve.

What's Wrong with Entrepreneurship?

As you'll see, there's a lot wrong with entrepreneurship, as institutionalized as it's become. To clarify, what Rafael did remains as exciting and rewarding as ever. He solved a problem he cared about that helped others enough that they rewarded him for it—what I call taking initiative. But he didn't start a company—what people usually mean by entrepreneurship today.

The popular mindset has demoted initiative below Dog Show Entrepreneurship, leading people like Rafael to stay in jobs they dislike longer instead of helping themselves and the people around them.

The media over-represent Dog Show Entrepreneurship in TV shows like *Shark Tank* and *Silicon Valley*, movies like *Steve Jobs* and *The Social Network*, and countless magazine and newspaper headlines. Our educational system favors it. They think they're serving everyone, but they're not. Traditional academic classes based on case studies, papers, and tests—but not active, experiential learning—don't help people *practice* entrepreneurship, as I'll describe in chapter 4.

Their practical courses are often based on unconscious biases that lead them to turn away most people they purport to help, probably including you. The biases appear in their applications to take the courses, which ask applicants for ideas and teams, based on and supporting a myth that projects have to begin with ideas. I call it the Myth of the Great Idea. It leads people who want to promote entrepreneurship to select for people in STEM fields, makers, tinkerers, researchers.

While many entrepreneurs are STEM types and many STEM types create ideas worth marketing, only 6 percent of all workers are in STEM jobs.[1] Our educational systems act as if the non-STEM applicants are a 6-percent niche to their market. I believe non-STEM people, and many STEM types who would love to initiate projects but don't have ideas and teams, are more like 94 percent of the market—woefully underserved, even pushed away and rejected by course applications, lingo, jargon, and other aspects of a Dog Show culture.

This barrier filters out people like Rafael and others outside STEM fields, while making Dog Show promoters feel like they're helping most aspiring entrepreneurs. On the contrary, most simply don't apply.

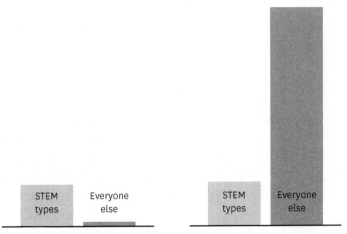

| The Dog Show view of demand for entrepreneurial training; mostly STEM people and a few non-STEM. | A more likey case, invisible to those who select only applicants with ideas and teams. |

The Myth of the Great Idea infects more than STEM fields. Social entrepreneurship programs promote it too. The bias appears in universities, government-run programs, incubators, co-working spaces, books, online courses, and throughout education. University programs evolved into similar government programs, including at the National Science Foundation and National Institutes of Health, which select applicants similarly.

Like many institutions, Dog Show Entrepreneurship tends to sustain itself, not necessarily entrepreneurs, however well-intentioned.

To be sure, it helps many who fall within its focus, but even then, what about those who competed and lost? Most deals offered on *Shark Tank* fall through. Far more aspirants don't make the show than do. They put in time distracted from customers, employees, and operations while preparing elevator pitches and glossy presentations with little to show for it.

What about the people dissuaded from trying? What about the people who try based on these inaccurate representations, only to flail in a world unlike their expectations? What does society lose in discouraging those who might work on problems that don't lend themselves to Dog Show solutions?

The net effect of this institutionalization may be to *lower* overall entrepreneurial activity.

I come across and teach people who emerged from such programs. They tell me the programs missed the human element they sought—connecting with *people*, developing as people themselves, and discovering and developing their passions, not just what will win a contest. Chris, an experienced entrepreneur you'll meet in Part Two who did this book's exercises, previously learned two methodologies—Lean and Design Thinking—that are popular in Silicon Valley, universities, and corporations. He told me,

> Method Initiative is what I would recommend as a first step on an entrepreneurial journey. The exercises get you out talking to people at the ideation stage and you start benefiting from their wisdom, and you also start seeding a network of support. Also, unlike Design Thinking or Lean, Method Initiative helps you gain clarity on what is right for you. Design Thinking helps you explore a problem space but it still doesn't start with what you love, or develop you. Lean helps you find product market fit for your business but it doesn't help you figure out what business to run or if you'll like it. Your exercises are prior to Design Thinking and Lean—to get you started when you don't know what you want to do and to start building that all-important network of support.

I'll talk more about such programs in chapter 4. They teach how to manage existing projects, which is important but doesn't teach you to initiate, as Rafael learned to, nor to examine your values and develop social and emotional skills to develop projects based on what you care about. Chris only realized what he missed when he learned something broader and more fundamental than entrepreneurship—to take initiative in general.

STEM communities often create solutions in search of problems. Starting with people and their problems relieves that problem.

JONATHAN

Jonathan was an Ivy-educated lawyer with a successful practice. He earned multiple six figures per year, but the money and the clients weren't exciting passion. He felt despondent.

His mentor suggested taking a class—any class—to help him get out of his doldrums. He ended up taking mine, with no expectation of starting a project.

I didn't know his background when he took my class. I only knew he was doing the exercises. He did the exercises and spoke about a non-profit he envisioned. It was still evolving when he finished the exercises. He continued talking to valuable people.

A few months after he finished the exercises, he updated me on the non-profit.

He partnered with a programmer from Harvard, where their project won an award.

They formed the non-profit—a website to simplify and dramatically lower the cost of bankruptcy to what low-income people could afford, effectively restoring their legal rights.

Jonathan and his team are helping people—hundreds so far, and more all the time. They have 5 stars on Yelp. On a grander scale, they're helping to restore an important check on capitalism. As a result, they've seen coverage in the *Washington Post*, the *Wall Street Journal*, *Forbes*, *Inc.*, and *TechCrunch*. They've received funding from the US government, Harvard, former Google CEO Eric Schmidt, and Facebook's Mark Zuckerberg.

The market's incumbent providers are noticing the competition. Jonathan is beyond helping a few people. He is disrupting an industry.

He didn't start with the intention of making waves. He didn't know he would create a project at all. His case illustrates that even if your goal is to become Best in Show, learning to find and love a dog that's perfect for you is the best way there.

Jonathan and his project keep succeeding. As this book goes to press, Y Combinator selected them and Jonathan to participate in their prestigious program. They received support from the Robin Hood Foundation, and the American Bar Association named his project one of the best web tools of 2018.

On a personal level, Jonathan loves his work. One person served by his non-profit wrote:

My wife [and I] can't thank you enough for helping us through our financial problems. We are now able to handle our monthly expenses and will be out of debt before long. If it wasn't for your guidance, we would still be paying very high interest rates and be further in debt. Although we are getting older and are in poor health, we don't have to look over our shoulders for collection agencies. You changed our lives. God bless you.

A far cry from doldrums with no direction.

I spoke to Jonathan about Method Initiative, which he describes as his turning point from lacking direction to the discovery of a passion. He told me he had no conscious access to this passion before he started, but it felt completely natural once he had a method to act on it.

He said, "What I really got out of it was the confidence that I can gain credibility and build something in basically any field. What I learned is that it's not about having the great, sexy idea, but about having a decent idea and then asking people experiencing the problem for their advice. That was really effective for me.

"I used to be very intimidated to talk to high-value experts," he explained. "I realized in taking this course that by approaching people with passion and enthusiasm for what they're doing, they were very willing to give not just feedback on my ideas but also direction on a lot of different ways of going, including different ideas.

"It's affected my confidence in reaching out to people because I realized that I can build anything. I can reach out to anyone and, within a very short period of time, I can go from zero in a space to becoming an insider and somebody who people respect and want to interact with."

And, as he said, there's nothing complicated about it. In his words, "It's 100-percent simple, 100-percent practical, 100-percent effective. There's just exercise, experience, reflection, and results."

Jonathan began his project as you will yours in the first few exercises—scratching an itch, examining a few problems, playing around with potential solutions. While you can't predict where they'll lead, you will nearly always find that the problems you find affect large numbers of people.

An earlier iteration of Jonathan's project was to consult with people in person. That iteration would have lowered some people's costs, but would not have disrupted a field. You'll generally have the option to pursue your solutions as deeply as you want, and you will often find that depth leading to fundamental social problems. Or not, if you don't feel the need to compete for Best in Show. There are as many ways to love a dog as there are dogs and owners.

The Dog Show Cabal

Understanding the people and institutions promoting Dog Show Entrepreneurship helps you understand what drives it. I call these people the Dog Show Cabal—though I don't mean they collude, only that they respond to similar incentives that tend to help each other. Let's review a few.

Shark Tank and its peers

Shark Tank describes itself as a "business-themed show that has become a culturally defining series and inspires a nation to dream bigger" and that has "reinvigorated entrepreneurship." Has it? Consider its motivations and follow the money.

The show and its peers succeed through ratings that bring in ad revenue, not necessarily through the entrepreneurial success of its contestants. Ratings come from drama, not from accuracy or helping aspiring entrepreneurs.

Shows like this imply that they are promoting entrepreneurship, but they present what attracts viewers—drama and vaudeville, however ineffective.

They don't present end results. *Forbes* has documented that most *Shark Tank* deals don't close.[2] The magazine "spoke to 237 of those business owners [of the 319 who accepted deals on-air in seven years] and discovered 73% did not get the exact deal they made on TV."

"What if I want exposure?" you might ask. Yes, there is value in it for some, as *Forbes* also reported that, for many of the contestants they reached, "the publicity of appearing on the show ended up being worth more than the deal." But thousands spent time on applications that distracted them from their customers, employees, and operations, but didn't make the show and received nothing for their time and effort.

If you want media attention, you will get more coverage by building your project, then figuring out which journalists and audiences will appreciate it. If you can show that you'll increase their audiences, ratings, or sales, you can approach members of the media with confidence. This book's exercises will show you how, through experience. Shooting the moon and hoping for the best are not effective strategies.

I'm not criticizing these shows for entertaining viewers, just considering their effect on entrepreneurship and initiative. Your project may not need investment, which would make these shows distractions that teach counterproductive habits. Investors will own part of your company, often for years. What if your personalities, visions, or styles don't match? Why force the entire process of meeting someone for the first time, teaching them about your business, proposing a deal, negotiating it, and deciding into a few minutes? What are these shows communicating when the contestants don't ask about the backgrounds of the investors? Even knowing it's staged, can you distinguish which practices on such shows will help your project and which are counterproductive? Business success comes from relationships based on people, not from performing for a camera in staged, unnatural contexts.

The media

The media in general also succeed through clicks, ratings, drama, Emmys, Oscars, celebrity, and ticket sales, not accuracy, effective education, satisfying customers, or your growth. Despite claiming to promote entrepreneurship, the media often portray founders as rock stars. They suggest that technology and innovation will create a brighter future and save us from disaster.

Sounds great, but again, follow the money. They're not primarily motivated to help you develop as a person, entrepreneur, or initiator, nor to help you serve your customers or operate your business. As Facebook co-founder Eduardo Saverin said of *The Social Network*, "The movie was clearly intended to be entertainment and not a fact-based documentary." And early Apple employee Bill Atkinson said of the movie *Steve Jobs*, "Not truthful at all. That wasn't his character, and the events didn't happen. You think of Jobs having a reality distortion field. I think of [writer] Aaron Sorkin as having... a history distortion field."

Venture capitalists

Venture capitalists and other institutional investors claim to support entrepreneurs, but their main goal is to return money to their investors. That money comes from somewhere. Entrepreneurs taking advice from VCs is like fish taking advice from fishermen. They'll advise you on how to grow, then on how to swim near their lures.

As a VC said to fellow VC and entrepreneur Paul Graham,[3] "Once you take several million dollars of my money, the clock is ticking." Graham clarified: "If VCs fund you, they're not going to let you just put the money in the bank and keep operating as two guys living on ramen. They want that money to go to work."

What Is a Venture Capitalist?

A venture capitalist, or VC, is a person or institution who invests in a business that the financial world considers riskier than most, due to reasons like inexperienced managers, untested products or services, untested operational models, unknown customer interest, unknown or high competition, or low access to adequate funding if the business succeeds.

In return for that risk, VCs expect a high return on investment, often within a few years. They gathered the money to invest in *you* by getting people to invest in *them*, promising them high returns. Not delivering jeopardizes their jobs and reputations.

They know that risk means many of their investments will fail and return nothing, so they need the ones that succeed to return colossal amounts—often ten or a hundred times their investment. So most venture capitalists only consider businesses with huge potential returns.

I include here individuals who are experienced, rich, and connected enough to act like institutional investors.

As Westminster suits some dog breeders, institutional investors are perfect for some entrepreneurs. They perform a critical role in the investment world, but interests can conflict.

Have you heard of Martin Eberhard? I hadn't either. You've probably heard of the product he created and the company he founded in 2003. His main investor ended up taking control of the company and squeezed him out so thoroughly that his name is little-known. But Eberhard founded Tesla after doing most of the work of developing its first car. You've probably heard of Elon Musk, who invested in the company a year later and forced Eberhard out to become CEO in 2008.

As *Business Insider* reported,[4] "The Tesla board had held a meeting without him, Eberhard said, and decided that it was time for him to go. 'There was no discussion,' Eberhard said. 'I didn't get to hear what they said. I didn't get to defend myself. I felt totally stranded...' Though he stayed on the board and remained on staff with the company, Martin was off everything but troubleshooting and tending to peripheral issues. He'd been shut out of the company he founded. The whole exchange was classic Musk, said [Mike] Harrigan, the VP of customer service and support who would become the VP of marketing."

In the article, Tesla's interim CEO said, "Martin is a very good technical guy, and he had a vision, but he wasn't a particularly good CEO." Musk and Tesla's board did what they considered best for the company, not necessarily for the man who did the most to start it.

I speak from experience. In 2003, investors squeezed me out of the first company I co-founded. I had never led a company before, let alone in a recession post tech bubble and post 9/11. We can't know how things might have gone differently, but the pain of the experience became one of my greatest motivations to teach initiative: to give people the skills, experiences, and beliefs to succeed beyond what any other resources can give them, before the stakes get high.

As for initiatives that won't generate large returns, like Rafael's or Jonathan's, institutional investors see them as distractions. If anything, they would likely have encouraged them to leave and start new companies to invest in, whether or not it would benefit them or anyone else.

Many venture capitalists will say that their worst investments are "lifestyle" businesses—that is, ones with enough profit for the founder to live a great lifestyle but not enough for the business to cash out. If they invest in you, they'd prefer your business expand or go bankrupt for the tax loss, whether you or your customers want it or not.

In other words, wanting a great lifestyle with a stable business you love and that serves your community puts you in conflict with venture capitalists.

As for initiatives not designed to generate profit—a non-profit, a community organization, or an opportunity for a promotion or raise, for example—you're wasting their time. My podcast is one of my life's great projects. I believe it will play a major role in solving our environmental problems, but it won't register on investors' radar. Decreasing consumption conflicts with their interests, however helpful it is environmentally. Many of my greatest role models— Henry David Thoreau, Nelson Mandela, Mohandas Gandhi, Martin Luther King Jr.—would not have gotten help from VCs and, in fact, may have gotten resistance.

Venture capitalists' main interests are:

- Finding businesses with the potential to return colossally more than they invested, within a few years, in cash
- Investing with terms as favorable to themselves as possible
- Leading the business to return the investment within a few years, in cash

If you believe venture capital will help you, you will usually be better off focusing on your customers, employees, and operations first, as well as personal interests like your happiness and enthusiasm, before pursuing VCs. The more stable and profitable your project, the more VCs will like it, the less you will need them, the more you'll attract them, and the better deals you'll be able to create.

Investing means negotiating a deal, and negotiation involves two parts: growing the pie and splitting it. The growing-the-pie part generally aligns your interests with theirs. The splitting-the-pie part puts theirs in conflict with yours. They're professionals, generally more experienced than the entrepreneurs they invest in. They may create a deal where you and other stakeholders lose while they win, so even a big investment that ensures the company's profitability can mean success for them at your expense.

The same conflict occurs when investors cash out. Your business may be thriving, but if it doesn't bring enough cash for VCs to return to their investors, they'll feel motivated to change your company to increase their return.

For example, did you ever wonder why Google adopted the motto "Don't be evil"?

A company with no incentive to do something people might consider evil wouldn't need to say it. Saying it suggests that Google feels that incentive. And not just anyone said it. The founders did in the company's IPO prospectus.

"What could be evil about searching?" you might ask. "Searching only helps people find what they're looking for, right?"

Your searches tell Google what you want, information that advertisers value and pay for. Google's founders originally wanted to help people find things, which alone isn't profitable. Investors want profit, so they influenced Google to change.

Whatever its founders' intent, to an accountant, Google became an advertising media company. Search *costs* them money. Ads and selling your data *make* them money.

Since advertisers pay more the more they know about you, and searching reveals personal, often private, details, Google's employees sensed the incentive to learn about and store people's personal information and to profit from it. Hence, "Don't be evil."

Such results aren't inevitable. Wikipedia and Craigslist could have shifted their focus from the communities they served to advertisers, but chose not to. Google's executives became richer than Wikipedia's and Craigslist's, but also had to testify before Congress on how they may have contributed to undermining the United States' democratic process, antitrust violations, and more repercussions that many might consider evil. Perhaps, as a result, Google keeps deprecating its use of the phrase, now almost a footnote in its code of conduct.[5]

I'm not suggesting right or wrong in Google's case, only pointing out that many companies face such dilemmas, and investment often limits founders' ability to act on their values. Google's search functionality seems as superior to its competition as Wikipedia's and Craigslist's functionality is to theirs. I wonder if Google's founders ever think about whether they could have served the world as effectively as Wikipedia and Craigslist without the problems that led to testifying before Congress. Craigslist's Craig Newmark is still reported to be a billionaire. (For what it's worth, I search with duckduckgo.com.)

Corporations

Many corporations, especially large ones, promote entrepreneurship among their employees, teaching it in training programs, for example. But they do so for the corporation's benefit, not necessarily the employees', as you'd expect from following the money.

I teach initiative and entrepreneurship to corporate teams in such programs. Their program managers often specify that participants' projects must benefit the company first, which can limit employees' optimal development. One program specifically wanted an "internal *Shark Tank*." My task on paper was to teach the participants, but as the program progressed, they asked me to focus on pitching the CEO—that is, teaching Dog Show skills.

I believe corporations would benefit more without that restriction, since it filters out people like Rafael. He could have learned to help the company as he did sooner and without seeking outside help.

Governments

Governments generally want economic growth, which not all initiative creates, including many social, political, and cultural initiatives. We call politicians leaders, but they tend to follow funding sources, voters, and media attention. They promote programs that help the industries that support them and generate votes. If your project meets their interests, government grants or connections can help, but government bureaucrats follow rules and avoid attention, controversy, and risk. They tend to move slowly.

Business plan competitions and pitch events

Pitch events and business plan competitions attract many aspiring entrepreneurs, enabling them to meet and pitch investors they might not otherwise have reached. Still, the investors spend time and money creating the event because they expect to make that money back. You're performing for them. They advise you to present based on what makes it easiest for them to choose, making you a commodity. They distract you from focusing on the communities you intend to serve. They motivate you to work on their schedules, not your market's. They create a relationship based on them judging you.

Many of my students have won awards, grants, and investment from such competitions. I recommend against focusing on them, which I think helps them win.

If you believe pitch events will help you, you will usually be better off focusing on your customers, employees, and operations first, as well as personal interests like your happiness and enthusiasm, before competing. The more stable and profitable your project, the more judges will like it, the less you will need them, the more you'll attract them, and the better deals you can create.

If funding is a mutually beneficial part of your project, you should be able to show the sponsors directly how you will help them and initiate relationships with them with confidence as an equal, not a contestant.

Dog Show Entrepreneurship Hurts Even If You Aren't in It

"But I'm not going for VC money or trying to work with the Dog Show Cabal. I don't have to worry, right?"

Whether you use them or not, they are influential on a cultural level. Here's why:

They teach us to think entrepreneurship requires elements of the Dog Show, like fast growth, pitch events, VC backing, fast returns, and transforming industries. We forget that the skills of entrepreneurship and initiative can enable us to start projects within companies that may earn us responsibilities, promotions, raises, independence, and passion. We lose sight of how we can start non-profits, community organizations, or even informal projects that nonetheless enrich our lives. Your managers or potential teammates might think this way and devalue your work.

They teach us to think entrepreneurship requires things we can't get, that entrepreneurs are born with special skills or talents, that they need conditions to be just right, that they need investors, and such. If we think entrepreneurship requires technology, investment, or a special process to start, what opportunities might we be missing?

They teach us to think the stakes are high. We see entrepreneurship as big and showy—its plans, successes, and failures. We think we have to do something big, profitable, or revolutionary.

They discourage us from starting. Many who would love to take the responsibility and initiative of starting a project, who could help others, and who could free themselves from onerous, compliance-based work don't do it. They think they need ideas or teams to start. They don't realize how many successful people and projects began from scratch. They fear their managers won't be receptive to their ideas. Most of all, they don't realize that they can develop skills to create ideas and attract team members.

They distance us from our passions. Not knowing how to take initiative leads people to live passionless lives, toeing the line. We look at Dog Show winners and conclude they must have been purebreds—that is, born with something special. We think successful people must have known their passions from the start to be able to devote themselves so much. We think, "Poor me. I don't know my passion. If I did, I'd do what they did, but what can I do but wait and hope it finds me?"

Dog Show Entrepreneurship rests on and propagates myths that discourage many from trying and that distract those who do, which I'll treat more fully in chapter 6. The myths support some populations, but people like Rafael, Jonathan, and others you'll meet in this book, whose successes belie those myths, exist outside that system.

It leads people to expect eager aspiring entrepreneurs to perform for them and the world—to coif themselves and trot jauntily.

It frames the field in its terms, taking advantage of its media reach.

It leads people to expect entrepreneurs to be young STEM types born with special skills, highly educated, outside big companies, and attracted to risk.

It leads people to believe that initiative and entrepreneurship means new ventures, leaving jobs to live on nothing, and so on.

It leads people only to start with big, perfect ideas and perfect pitches.

The Dog Show removes options, as Rafael and Jonathan felt. Fewer options means less pay, fewer promotions, less responsibility, and doing what you're told, for everyone. You have fewer opportunities to propose projects. Even if you see opportunities, others become less receptive.

Fewer options means you see less opportunity at work and in life. You feel less able to help yourself or others. You may not see problems you could solve. Helplessness makes people more dependent, complacent, compliant, and unhappy. Fewer options means living more by others' values, powering systems that enrich them and control you. It means stagnation.

Many more people say they want to act with initiative than do. For decades I've asked such people why they haven't taken initiative. Their top answer is not having a great idea, a myth that the Dog Show Cabal propagates but history disproves. Many great initiators began without great ideas, and so can you. In Part Two, I will teach you to replicate their success.

My students and clients come from all fields, ages, and interests, and they are thriving with the projects they created outside Dog Show Entrepreneurship.

[handwritten: Personal Narrative]

*[handwritten: * descriptive detail]*

JOSHUA, PART 1

[handwritten: , setting]

A decade before I worked with Rafael, I felt trapped in graduate school, despite being a poster boy for succeeding at what society told me meant success. I was on track to earn my fourth Ivy League degree—a PhD in a STEM field with a well-connected advisor on a groundbreaking experiment.

My future looked bright from the outside. My advisor was prominent and well-connected. I was helping build a satellite that would produce data for a thesis that would get me hired. Students from my team would go on to post-docs at NASA, Harvard, Caltech, Columbia, and other renowned institutions. I should have felt prepared to take on the world.

Instead I felt I had few options, and didn't like any of them. Looking out from my dingy shared office last renovated during the space race or maybe the Manhattan Project, I envied everyone else. They enjoyed their work. They went out for drinks with coworkers and had fun after work. They could leave their work behind when they left the office. They made more money and had more chances to advance. People admired them for their work. Their offices had been designed after the '60s.

That's what I thought anyway. Meanwhile, I'd lost my passion for astrophysics. I wondered if I'd loved it in the first place. I'd hoped making it my profession would reignite something.

It didn't.

On the contrary, it undermined and quashed that passion. I was doing what others told me to based on their interests, not initiating based on mine.

I thought there was something wrong with me.

I considered my options. First, I could keep doing what I was doing. The work may have been long and hard, but it followed a dependable path requiring no personal challenge or risk. But I had exhausted my motivation.

Second, I could go into industry. The work would be easier and the pay greater, but I saw it as entering a military-industrial complex, which I didn't want to do.

Third, I could go to Wall Street. The work would be yet easier, the pay yet greater, and the path more clear, but I found the culture unattractive.

Then I got lucky. In the '90s dot-com boom (not yet called a bubble), entrepreneurship was in the news. Two college friends, Matt and Jeremy, told me they were dissatisfied with their work and had met a few times to come up with an idea for a startup. They hadn't come up with anything and decided to bring me in.

I had so far had little exposure to entrepreneurship, nor interest in it. On the contrary, I associated business with the 1989 Exxon Valdez oil spill, and so avoided it. Einstein, my role model, said about money, "The example of great and pure individuals is the only thing that can lead us to noble thoughts and deeds... Can anyone imagine Moses, Jesus, or Gandhi armed with the moneybags of Carnegie?"

But Jeremy and Matt were great friends of mine so I joined the team. In 1996, I thought of an idea with potential. Jeremy moved to Boston to get married but Matt and I began developing the technology. In 1998 we filed for a patent. It cost more than we could afford so we started looking for investment.

The dot-com-bubble media celebrated high-profile entrepreneurs like rock stars and created a Dog Show culture, which I absorbed out of inexperience. As far as I knew, I was bound to become a hero founder-CEO.

Columbia's business school was next door to the physics building so I found and took entrepreneurship classes there. I still wanted to keep my physics options open, however depressing, so I persuaded the professors to let me audit their classes without registering. Business school culture reflected Dog Show culture.

November 1999 marked several major milestones. I defended my thesis, moved to a new apartment away from Columbia, and our company got its first funding. We got our first big contract in 2000, debuted in Atlanta in 2001 and in New York City in 2002, and soon after expanded to Hong Kong, Tokyo, Budapest, Athens, and Mexico City. Investors came in at over $10 million in valuations.

A storybook ending, right?

Sadly not. Despite being a brick-and-mortar company with satisfied customers, the bursting of the dot-com bubble decimated our revenue and potential for investment. September 11 security measures increased time and costs for installations in the United States. We teetered on bankruptcy.

My Dog Show Entrepreneurship education that came amid the dot-com bubble didn't prepare me to lead a team through such times. I cried out of frustration, helplessness, and lost dreams more than once. So much for the hero founder-CEO.

By 2003, unable to handle the company's debt, I had the choice of accepting bankruptcy for the company or the investors' terms, which included replacing me as CEO. In a low point of my life, to cement my ouster, when the new CEO and remaining team moved to smaller offices, they simply didn't give me a key.

THE DOG SHOW
AND CULTURE

While the following chapter is not necessary to learning initiative, I offer it both as a way to begin restoring the spirit of initiative that helped found the nation I live in, and to do my part in helping to solve some of our world's great problems. The purely practical reader can skip this chapter, but for those willing to invest a few more moments, I hope it offers some motivation.

WE LIVE IN challenging times.

Crises abound: the environment, terrorism, racism, widening gaps between rich and poor, campus strife, plastic choking our oceans, global warming, opioids, nuclear weapons, political and economic polarization, and so on, all abetted by 24-hour news and social media addicting viewers with fear and outrage.

People with the skills, experience, and beliefs to solve such problems, however unwanted, see these crises as an opportunity to help.

Our society, sadly, is developing fewer such initiators. As with sports, where we create a few superstars while over 70 percent of the population is overweight or obese, our society promotes Dog

Show Entrepreneurship from grade school to university and corporate training. The motivation seems to make sense: since existing solutions don't work, we need new ones, which means innovation, which means technology, which means entrepreneurship, which means the Dog Show.

But the Dog Show often undermines and stifles what would help society in favor of what helps a few investors.

Take health care, for example, where you'd expect technology to help. Few, if any, technological innovations can match the results of unprofitable initiatives like checklists for doctors or basic sanitation. In 2009, the *New York Times* quoted the *New England Journal of Medicine*:[1] "'Surgical complications are a considerable cause of death and disability around the world... They are devastating to patients, costly to health care systems and often preventable.' But a year after surgical teams at eight hospitals adopted a 19-item checklist, the average patient death rate fell more than 40 percent and the rate of complications fell by about a third, the researchers reported."

A 40-percent reduction in death rates is spectacular—nearly unprecedented—yet it needed no technology or investment. Why did we wait until 2009 for a solution needing nothing more than a pencil and paper?

Checklists start like my dog, Jake—labors of love. Outside the Dog Show, though, the world may love a Jake more than a conformation show winner.

How many people impassioned to help others spend decades chasing Dog Show dreams, missing their Jakes? How much faster could medicine have implemented checklists with a system less enthralled by the Dog Show? How many lives were lost in the process?

On sanitation, Florence Nightingale's advances in cleanliness required no technology beyond keeping statistics, yet saved more lives than possibly any billion-dollar drug and continue to save lives around the world at nearly no cost. She loved her Jake.

Industries make billions off fad diets and bottled water, yet almost nothing off broccoli and tap water, despite how these things promote health and avoid pollution.

I have no problem with people wanting to start the next Facebook. In fact, Jonathan's results illustrate that the exercises in Part Two that helped Rafael with his Jake can equally create a Best in Show. Method Initiative also produces results like checklists and sanitation, despite how our culture doesn't support such efforts nearly as much.

Many of our time's crises, including its biggest, are fundamentally social. Dog Show solutions don't often solve social problems. Initiative that puts the people with the problem first does.

Consider our environmental problems. Many people, especially those in the Dog Show, put faith in technology to solve these problems, to the exclusion of other innovations. History, economics, and systems thinking show technology and efficiency exacerbating problems.

If the idea of efficiency and technology causing problems sounds backward, let's go back to the start of many of our environmental concerns. If anything marked the beginning of the industrial revolution, James Watt's steam engine did. It wasn't the first steam engine, but was more efficient than any before it.

More efficient means using less energy and creating less pollution, right?

Sadly, no. Each engine used less coal, yes, but as a result, more people used more engines, and for more purposes, so engines collectively used more coal overall and polluted more than before.

In economics terms, the place to look for the effect of efficiency is the demand curve, not in particular existing uses. If the demand curve slopes downward, lower prices mean more use. LEDs use less energy than incandescents and now we're lighting things more and lighting more things, on track to use more energy than ever. As incandescents did when they supplanted whale oil, as adding lanes and roads increased traffic, as gas engine efficiencies led to bigger cars rather than improved mileage, our global economic system produces and increases environmental problems.

Over centuries the trend is clear: we are more efficient than ever and polluting more than ever as a result. In many markets, and globally overall, efficiency leads to more use, which pollutes more, which drives more efficiency, creating a self-reinforcing cycle. One result is material abundance. Another is today's polluted world. In the words of researchers at MIT and the Center of Economic Research at ETH Zurich,[2] "long-run energy-saving technological change has increased energy efficiency, which in turn has promoted energy use. The potential reduction in energy use from energy efficiency improvements (i.e., the energy savings) has been overcompensated by the energy services response (i.e., the energy rebound)."

Technology, innovation, and efficiency helped us as long as their lower prices and increased production outweighed the costs of increased output. Until recently, few saw downsides with increased production and pollution.

For centuries, we could debate or even dismiss the evidence that humans could affect the planet on a global scale.

Now the evidence is overwhelming that we did, and it will accelerate if we don't act decisively. No one need pretend otherwise. Even amid disagreements in some areas, we're projected to have more plastic than fish in the Pacific Ocean by 2050. Nobody wants mercury in their fish. We're seeing extinctions moving faster than ever seen over billions of years. You've read the headlines.

If you believe that technological improvements will suddenly change their overall effects after centuries of this consistent trend, you're dreaming.

People believe self-serving myths in the face of abundant countervailing evidence, probably because they prefer comfort and convenience over stewarding the environment. Making a system designed for overproduction more efficient will cause it to overproduce more efficiently.

To think electric cars, solar power, nuclear power, a hyperloop train system, and so on will lower pollution in the long term ignores history. Ride-hailing apps like Uber and Lyft, predicted to lower miles driven and pollution, have increased congestion and miles driven. Their efficiency enables people to ride more and more people to ride.

You don't get out of trouble by following the principles that got you into it.

Making a System More Efficient Achieves Its Goals More

Steam engines, LEDs, nuclear reactors, and technology in general are elements of a system. Even the economy is an element of a global system that includes the environment and other subsystems.

The goals of this overall system include growth, externalizing costs, and individual comfort and convenience, not enjoying what we have or responsibility for how our actions affect others—all the consequences of our actions, not just those we want. As long as we pursue growth, externalizing costs, comfort, and convenience over appreciating what we have and personal responsibility, Dog Show Entrepreneurship and technological innovation will drive those goals.

Our culture took generations to learn that building more roads increased traffic, congestion, pollution, time lost, and so on. Parts of the infrastructure we built will endure for centuries, along with the traffic, congestion, pollution, time lost, and so on.

Myths that solar planes and other efficiencies—without cultural shifts like changing systemic goals—will lower overall pollution locks in more damage.

Different results mean changing our behavior. Making our current system more efficient won't fix our greatest problems. It will achieve them more efficiently.

Changing the beliefs and goals of a system can change it. Cultures have done so before. We can do it again. Cultural change comes from people-based initiative, rarely the Dog Show.

We've changed cultural beliefs about drunk driving, smoking, racial equality, seat belts, ozone, and leaded gas, for example. I remember as a child hearing people say, "Give me one for the road," meaning, "I'm about to drive, please give me alcohol." Our culture has largely shunned the beliefs behind "one for the road." Cigarettes used to evoke Humphrey Bogart, now they evoke cancer. Car safety used to be an afterthought, now it's a critical sales feature. The book *Unsafe at Any Speed* may have led to more lives saved than any technological innovation from within the industry. It changed systemic beliefs. New beliefs, even tempering enthusiasm for technology, don't mean slowing innovation—just redirecting it, as progress with air bags, crumple zones, and so on attest.

Initiatives like slow food, minimalism, and zero waste, and initiators like Rosa Parks, Rachel Carson, and Harvey Milk seem to the Dog Show Cabal like Jake would to Westminster, yet improve and even save lives, as checklists for doctors and Florence Nightingale's sanitation did.

There is a place for the Dog Show. Sometimes someone finds a mold that inhibits bacterial growth and we need investment to develop and produce antibiotics. Likewise, once we change our system's goals, technical innovation can help people, as with car safety. Before *Unsafe at Any Speed*, automotive engineers made cars less safe. After, more.

I don't pretend to have the key for solving our greatest problems. But imagine a shift like in automotive safety happening around today's problems. Today's drug companies profit from opioid addiction and contribute to it. Imagine the reverse. Why do we study Rosa Parks if not to emulate her?

THE SOLUTION, PART 1
INITIATIVE

DAVID

David was an illustrator in a Spanish animation studio aspiring to direct when he approached me and we started working together. He had the skills to advance and the directors and producers were moving toward promoting him, but he viewed advancing in his career as transactional—an impersonal change in a corporate hierarchy. This view was a problem for someone who wanted to direct movies, where your voice has to come through, requiring expressing yourself openly.

He also feared that his illustrator peers thought he was trying to rise above them, and that fear held him back. Would they resent him?

We worked on his relationships with the directors and producers at his studio. Instead of seeing asking for a promotion as a transaction, he learned to ask advice, and to learn their problems and interests so he could help solve them.

The result: they promoted David to co-direct *Tad the Lost Explorer and the Secret of King Midas*, which set Spanish box office records and established a movie franchise. He has walked on red carpets around the Spanish-speaking world, though he is by nature a reserved person.

*I like the "lesson" he learned
and become better,*

How did these results happen? In his words, he learned how "to connect with the directors and producers as people, not 'bosses' or 'authorities.'" Instead of working *for* them, he's working *with* them ... "which is more productive, rewarding, and fun."

Beyond the money and accolades, he made himself an equal member of an accomplished creative team of former bosses. Bosses rarely take initiative to bring you into their inner circles. They're busy working on their careers. By contrast, they welcome people who take initiative to solve problems in ways that improve their lives and communities.

When the production ended, several of the former illustrator peers that he ended up directing went out of their way to say they liked working with him personally. Just as he had gone out of his way to connect personally with them while he was directing.

As this book goes to press, the studio re-signed him for the next film in the franchise, and he is working on various solo projects that he initiated.

David did what Rafael did: he learned a way to take initiative, to connect with people, and to solve people's problems so well that they rewarded him for it.

What We Could Have

Why did David hold back at first? Why don't we all create more productive relationships with the decision-makers who could promote or support us? How can we move from making excuses to embracing challenge?

Why do some people love what they do while others languish for years, sometimes for entire careers? Why do some people get promoted faster?

People's excuses rarely jibe with what works with successful initiators.

A popular excuse is not having a great idea, yet most founders started with poor ideas. Many of my students and clients started with none.

Another is not having resources, yet many successful initiators started with few resources, some with none. Guy Laliberté's Cirque du Soleil, which made him a billionaire, evolved from low- or no-budget street performances.

Another is lacking passion, but successful initiators couldn't have had passion for projects before those projects existed. They developed their passions along the way, as will you.

Another is fearing regret from choosing the wrong idea, yet most initiators' greatest successes come from later projects, not their first.

Another is saying they'll start later, but nearly all initiators say they wish they had started earlier.

What people who haven't started fear is what successful initiators embrace.

Knowing how to handle challenging situations leads you to look forward to what others fear and avoid, including what you feared in the past. It turns what you consider the worst of life into what you find the best. Imagine a life with enthusiasm replacing fear.

The results of mastering initiative include never having to suffer at work, knowing you can improve most situations, complaining less, and learning about the world, people, and yourself.

Passion will increase throughout your life as you learn to sense your interests and emotions, as well as those of people around you. You will find and create more meaning, value, importance, and purpose in your relationships and in what you do.

You will connect to your role models and feel connected to initiators throughout history. Your friendships and most of your relationships will improve. You will become more friendly with coworkers and colleagues, which will include more CEOs and people who could help your pursuits.

You will take responsibility for improving your situation and hold yourself accountable. You will lose the fallbacks of complaining and making excuses. You will lose tolerance for others complaining. You may lose friends who complain too much for you, but you will gain new ones who share more values with you. You may lead some complaining friends to join you.

None of the above has to cost much money. People will reward you for solving their problems. You'll build supportive communities.

There are caveats to these benefits: the results come from work and practice. No work, no results. No practice, no results.

The work is physically easy but socially and emotionally challenging. Feeling you want to give up socially or emotionally is different from wanting to give up physically. If you've never faced it, a big challenge awaits you. Many never overcome the feelings of wanting to give up socially or emotionally. But you can. There's a way: Method Initiative. It works.

Passion and Vulnerability

I've used the word *passion* a lot. You soon will too. To clarify, by passion I mean intense emotion, as in, "I feel passion for teaching," and the objects of that emotion, as in, "The *Leadership and the Environment* podcast is a passion of mine." Speaking of a thing's meaning, value, importance, or purpose is shorthand for the emotions it evokes. Feeling passion for something means it is meaningful, valuable, important, and purposeful.

Passions are what lead us to jump out of bed, call strangers who can help, and love doing grunt work for. However despondent, lethargic, discouraged, and depressed we may feel at times, we all have passions—that is, we all care about some things intensely.

To have a passion doesn't necessarily make you feel good, especially if you don't know how to act on it. Feeling passion without knowing how to act on it can make us feel powerless, so we often hide passions, even from ourselves.

Passions make us vulnerable. Others knowing what we care about opens us to manipulation and hurt. We've all been made fun of. Our hearts weren't broken by casual acquaintances but by people we cared for. The more we cared, the more we hurt.

So we learned to protect ourselves. When kids taunted us in the schoolyard for something we didn't care about, we could get rid of that thing. I remember kids teasing me for a shirt in high school. I never wore the shirt again. Problem solved.

What we couldn't get rid of—deep passions—we learned to protect, often by hiding. I remember kids taunting me in school for doing well in science and math. I did my best to hide these things, but couldn't. Problem not solved. Only years later, well into college, did I develop the strength and resolve to stop hiding my love for physics, and to major in it. Even then, again it was only years later that I become comfortable with it.

Hiding passions protects us, but also leads to a passionless life. By adulthood, many of us settle for going to work every day, talking about weather, sports, traffic, the market, and other things we feel no passion for, instead of what we care about. We suppress our passions because it's easier to sleep at night believing that we have no passion than to accept that we've given up on our dreams. Or that we *can* make the world a better place with something we feel passion for but *don't*. Many of us have told ourselves these stories for so long that we believe them. We believe we have no passions.

Seeing entrepreneurs and other initiators achieve greatness from nothing conflicts with such stories. When someone does what our story said was impossible, maintaining our protections requires telling ourselves more stories, like that they had unseen advantages, were born rich, or had connections we didn't. We think, "Oprah Winfrey [or whoever] must have been born with more empathy than me. If only I had been born so lucky, I'd have succeeded in my passion too, then I could have achieved what she did." Never mind the initiative she took, how hard she worked, or that she kept achieving beyond her show.

We think, "Martin Luther King Jr. and Nelson Mandela lived in times of great injustice. If I did too, then I would have worked against injustices. Even if I didn't reach their level, I'd at least have worked for the struggle." ℚ

Would you have?

I recently spoke to Beatrice Fihn, who is working to outlaw nuclear weapons. Does she have a chance? I can't say, but I hope so. She took initiative. Despite starting with no special advantage,

Can a role model have a special advantage?

she won the Nobel Peace Prize. Winning a Nobel Prize isn't completing the project, but it shows that valuable people support her. She loves her work, giving her life purpose and meaning.

After I read his memoir, *Born Standing Up*, Steve Martin became one of my favorite examples and personal inspirations. Why? Partly because he made millions of people laugh. He performed with an authenticity and genuineness that advanced his craft. He was the first comedian to fill stadiums. He didn't stop there. He moved to other arts: theater, music, film, essays, books, and more.

I count him as a role model mainly for succeeding with no great advantages nor having to overcome a crucible—no rich parents, family connections, or blatant injustices to fix. He took initiative, which led him to find and act on ever deeper and greater passions, then to take more initiative, then to the top of field after field. As far as I know, he loves performing and expressing his truth, which he does. He lives the motto: "Be so good they can't ignore you."

Comparable role models abound. Whoopi Goldberg won an Emmy, Grammy, Oscar, and Tony and hasn't slowed down. Results like hers come from initiative.

You can reach that level of your version of success. You don't have to solve all the world's problems or dismantle apartheid. You don't have to win Best in Show. You only have to develop the skills to find your Jake and to love and support him so he loves you back. Then repeat. That is, you need only develop the skills to find a problem you care about, affecting people you care about, and to solve it so that they reward you for it enough to sustain you. Then repeat.

Each time you do it, you'll develop the skills more, leading you to sense deeper, more meaningful passions. Unlike dogs, your projects don't have to be your responsibility for their whole lives. You can hand them to others and start new ones. I still meet with friends who kept working on projects we collaborated on but that I moved on from. Those projects led me to my greatest passions of today.

That's initiative.

So why haven't we learned it? Shouldn't schools teach it? As it turns out, they're trying. They're just trying in ways that don't work.

OUR MISGUIDED
EDUCATIONAL SYSTEM

JOSHUA, PART 2

As much as entrepreneurship saved me from the grind that mainstream education leads to, my Dog Show Entrepreneurship expectations sank me too.

I took years to recover financially and emotionally from being squeezed out of my first company. When I did, I realized I wanted to start new ventures, despite the pain of my first. I thought my best way to avoid similar shortcomings was a full MBA, so I went back to Columbia and earned one.

In business school, many classmates told me they wanted to start companies and took classes in entrepreneurship, but few were actually starting companies. It seemed entrepreneurship classes weren't working for them.

I felt disillusioned at the ineffectiveness of the entrepreneurship resources I found, including a place I spent tens of thousands of dollars and four semesters of my life. I also saw that successful initiators and entrepreneurs continued to arise without school, many specifically *leaving* school to greater success than those who finished.

These contradictions inspired me to reflect on an arc of lessons I learned from this part of my life:

1. Following the mainstream path often leads to a grind.
2. Initiative offers a way out, creating tremendous life options.
3. No existing resources teach you how to do it.
4. Some people learn to do it.
5. If they can, I can, and if I can, anyone can.
6. People believe they can't when they can.

I saw the potential to teach everyone how to do what great initiators did, uninhibited by the myths that the Dog Show perpetuated. I only had to create techniques to teach the effective development patterns in the fifth of these life lessons—"If they can, I can"—that schools and other resources missed, and to overcome the limiting beliefs of life lesson six—"People believe they can't when they can"—which I did.

Our Most Educated Are Often the Least Skilled

My feeling trapped and helpless in graduate school is sadly common. Many of the most educated feel the most trapped and helpless.

I've learned to highlight this shortcoming of our educational system in a talk I've given to many highly educated students and professionals. I first gave it to Columbia's medical school. A graduate student there who saw how much I loved working outside my PhD field invited me to speak to a student-run group there called the 92 Club, named because 8 percent of students in his field got jobs in what they studied. The other 92 percent had to fend for themselves.

I spoke to a full room of 150 people, including graduate students, post-docs, and researchers. I told them about the same the struggles I related in "Joshua, Part 1"—how I saw only three options, liked none, and felt trapped.

I asked them if they could relate.

One said, "Yes, that's why we brought you here." The room generally agreed.

I continued, "You've all heard of people who dropped out of school, like Bill Gates and Mark Zuckerberg, to start their own projects, right?"

They had.

I said, "You know that they could go in any direction they wanted as far as they wanted, right?"

They did.

I said, "You have *more* education but feel you have *fewer* options." I paused to let that sink in, then continued, "Isn't that the *opposite* of what an education is for?"

Every audience I ask this question, whether students or working professionals, reacts as dumbfounded. They need time to process how their education is leading to the opposite of their goal. They all show the same disillusionment as they look for what they misunderstood about education. I know I have their attention for the next hour.

Why do students and graduates of top programs at top universities feel trapped? Why did so many successful people leave school to succeed?

Anxiety pervades our educational system at every level, often in proportion to *meeting* its goals—that is, by design. Long-term research of grade-school students found that "suburban, relatively affluent... children of well-educated, white collar professionals... 'privileged' youth" show "significantly higher rates of drug use, depression, and anxiety than their lower income counterparts."[1] Why is more of our educational system producing more anxiety?

I don't leave the audience hanging, by the way. I tell them how taking initiative to start my first venture liberated me from feeling trapped by giving me the skills to start other new projects. I add that their school or employer won't likely teach them how, but they can learn themselves.

What's Wrong with Schools?

The academic information schools teach is nice, but the behavior they teach is compliance. Writer and former Yale professor William Deresiewicz aptly titled his book on what results from creating compliant people filled with facts but not social and emotional development: *Excellent Sheep.*

Greg Whiteley, director of the documentary *Most Likely to Succeed*, described the results of his interviewing many heads of companies, who told him:[2] "Kids who had come from the very best high schools and had gone on to the very best universities and graduated at the top of their class, when they come to us, frequently they were incapable of doing the work."

Whiteley described our educational system leading its most successful students to choose safe and predictable routes, studying safe and predictable subjects, losing touch with their passions, jettisoning ambition, and replacing asking "What do I love?" with "What does the teacher want and how can I give it to them?"

He said, "When you get into the real world to an employer like Google, like Cisco, or like any other startup, or any other company for that matter, and somebody says, 'Hey, I've got a problem. You're perfect. You've got this MBA, you graduated top of your class. You've never received anything less than an A. Take on this problem,' frequently these kids look at this problem, turn back to the employer—their boss—and say, 'Great! I can't wait to get started on this. Can you tell me how to do it?'"

That is, our top academic performers follow instructions well but need someone to tell them what to do. Is that what you want for yourself?

Whiteley continued, "These companies have revamped their hiring practices. Google is a great example. They no longer require a college diploma. They say that the number one predictor of success at the company is not how well you did in school, that there's zero correlation with how well you did in school and how good an employee you are. The number one predictor of success is if you

Independent work ethic

Internal

started a company before you got there, regardless of whether the company succeeded or not."

People feel anxious when they feel helpless to make a difference on something they care about.

The most viewed TED talk is on the failures of our educational system: "Do Schools Kill Creativity?" by Ken Robinson, with over 70 million views. Presidents and elected officials of every country prioritize education, but the sad result is that our educational system probably failed in teaching you how to take initiative.

Notable initiators who left our educational system include Bill Gates, Oprah Winfrey, Steve Jobs, Richard Branson, Mark Zuckerberg, Erin Brockovich, Elon Musk, Sean Combs, Lauryn Hill, Michael Dell, Whoopi Goldberg, Larry Page, and Sergey Brin, to name a few. Why did they choose to leave it? Each case is unique, but they left for something, not to play hooky. They sensed school would hold them back.

You may have had a few inspirational teachers, but schools mostly test how well you can recall facts and analyze abstract concepts. Teachers learn to teach what they're measured on, so most teach academic, impractical skills. Professors may spend lessons defining and categorizing entrepreneurship, initiative, and people who practice them. But academic skills don't help you take initiative or responsibility, nor do they build your self-awareness or ability to express yourself authentically and genuinely. Classroom learning doesn't help you develop the social and emotional skills underlying initiative and entrepreneurial success or personal development.

What is the point of education if not to teach students to improve their lives? What behavior do schools teach?

Everybody in the system may want to help students, but schools teach compliance through coercion, from kindergarten through university: when to attend, what to do, how to do it, with whom to do it, what subjects to take, how you will be measured, and so on. At university you may choose a major, but from a list, which tells you what courses to take.

Schools don't teach the social and emotional skills that enable students to succeed. They teach students to take tests, write papers, and comply. Social and emotional skills enable you to create meaning, value, importance, purpose, and passion in yourself and others. They enable you to communicate and behave genuinely and authentically. They enable self-awareness. Coercion, compliance, and abstract academic practices inhibit them.

Consider Rafael. Why did someone with an MBA not see the potential to improve his situation when a few months of coaching—including only a few hours of direct interaction with a coach—enabled him to transform his life?

He's not alone. Why do so many other well-educated people helplessly accept similar limitations? What do degrees and test scores mean if they don't prepare you to handle such common situations? What is our educational system missing?

Our educational system claims to teach entrepreneurship through its courses, degrees, and business plan competitions with cash prizes. But if entrepreneurship is so rewarding, why offer cash prizes? Do other fields offer cash to pursue them? Who is offering it and what do they want in return? How does that money influence the schools and universities that accept it? How does it influence the students who compete for it? What about non–Dog Show initiative?

What does money unrelated to operations teach students about solving problems and finding resources when that money is not available? What does it imply about the entrepreneurial playing field to other aspiring entrepreneurs when our top universities offer such advantages to their students? Might they discourage entrepreneurship overall?

What about students whose projects don't need investment? Many of them still apply for the competitions, learning to inflate their projects and put the interests of third-party judges before those of the people their projects serve.

Do grades and working on a school's schedule conflict with how students serve their customers and employees? If so, might that conflict suggest why so many successful people leave school?

Institutions Institutionalize

No entrepreneur became great by publishing academic papers, but professors publish or perish—all the more the more prestigious the university. They can't teach practical initiative from experience.

Universities' interests conflict with those of students who want to succeed through practical initiative and responsibility. They are academic institutions. Academic means distinct from practice and vocation. Vocation means a calling or passion. Institutions tend to institutionalize. They make their money through tuition, which motivates them to keep students enrolled, not to forge their own paths.

Their main deliverable is a credential—a transcript—more than knowledge or skills. Don't believe me? See what happens when you don't pay. Universities will let you finish your courses but they won't release your diploma and GPA. How useful is academic achievement if it doesn't stand on its own without a credential?

Credential comes from the Latin word for belief or trust. A credential like a transcript says, "Trust us that this graduate is good." Good at what, though? Increasingly people realize it means good at complying. Some fields may value compliance, but not entrepreneurship or initiative.

There are parts of education where academic credentials don't matter, for example, performance-based fields such as art, music, sports, the military, and leadership. Nobody hires actors, pianists, or other performers for their GPAs. They hire them for their abilities to perform.

Likewise, nobody will buy your product or service, join your team, invest in you, or support your project because of your GPA.

They'll support you if you perform, which in entrepreneurship means helping solve their problem. Credentials don't substitute for getting to know someone, making them feel comfortable enough to share their problems with you, and then solving those problems.

Universities' focus on credentials promotes a culture of padding them—more club memberships, more majors and minors, and so on. But more entries mean less depth, which conflicts with finishing things, learning deeply, and experiencing fully. How many companies did Bill Gates, Sam Walton, or Mark Zuckerberg start?

Some schools and universities have stopped teaching compliance, at least in entrepreneurship. Sadly, even among them problems persist.

Professors didn't perish, which means they published. They may have enjoyed or valued publishing, but did it give them relevant experience to help students? On the contrary, most developed skills irrelevant and counterproductive for entrepreneurship.

Music teachers who can't play music tend to teach music appreciation. If you want to learn to play music, classes in music appreciation may not hurt, but they don't help either. Entrepreneurship teachers who have only published papers teach entrepreneurship appreciation. Their classes may not hurt, but they don't help you practice entrepreneurship.

My student Nikita, whom you'll meet in Part Two, told me, "After my project in your class took off, I got more interested in entrepreneurship so I took another class in it. All they did was tell us the different roles of VCs and entrepreneurs. I learned all that from doing the project in your class. They didn't help us *do* anything."

I belonged to a committee of professors genuinely intending to help students by promoting entrepreneurship. In one meeting they proposed bringing in more big companies to promote corporate internships. At the same meeting they remarked that the web page development was slow because they couldn't find a company to code it. This was a school for engineers. They didn't see that they could use their own students, or didn't trust them, maybe for lacking the credentials they valued as academics themselves. Despite their best intent, they turned what could have helped students into exercises in compliance and institutionalization.

I once heard a leadership professor say he taught leadership theory only, not practice. Since I couldn't think of any leaders who led in theory but not practice, I tried to figure out what teaching only leadership theory produced. I only came up with teaching more leadership theory. I can imagine generations of leadership theory professors forming their own journals and departments but not leading or helping others. The same follows for teaching only entrepreneurship theory, which many professors do.

Many professors want to create centers and institutes. They institutionalize entrepreneurship, inhibiting its practice. Universities used to hire adjunct faculty with professional experience and skills to overcome what academic faculty lacked, but the trend now is to use adjuncts as part-time professors, decreasing this professional-world contribution.

Many universities provide extracurricular entrepreneurship programs, business plan competitions, and such, often funded by members of the Dog Show Cabal. The outcome is almost always a Dog Show event like a pitch day. University-based programs and pitch days arguably decrease student entrepreneurial activity and success by fostering Dog Show cultures. They publicize winners, and even those who didn't win might benefit from it, but those are selection effects. What about the rest of campus? Might non-participants learn to see entrepreneurship as a Dog Show spectacle? What about students with projects like Jake—perfect for them but with no chance of winning? These contests teach many students to force their projects to conform to the high-growth, fast-return, for-profit companies VCs like.

What about Lean and Design Thinking?

Two popular and successful methodologies for developing products are Lean and Design Thinking, which Chris described. Lean is a methodology for entrepreneurial management. Design Thinking teaches how to see, think, and interact on concepts and things related to design. Both are valuable in their domains and many entrepreneurs use them, but they teach skills different from taking initiative. They come later. For those who want to initiate from scratch, they help less. I'll treat Lean in detail, but this treatment applies similarly to Design Thinking.

Lean, in entrepreneurship, derives from Lean manufacturing and Lean production, which derive from management principles and practice from Toyota and other companies. Eric Ries's book *The Lean Startup* and Steve Blank's Lean LaunchPad Stanford course codified and popularized it.

Lean has produced many successes. Dropbox and Intuit use it, as do thousands of entrepreneurs and smaller companies. Hundreds of thousands of people have followed the book and course.

It continues to grow. Large companies use it to act more entrepreneurially. Universities nationwide use it. The National Science Foundation and National Institutes for Health promote it. The Federal Chief Information Officer of the United States has used it in government. The US federal government promotes it overseas.

 Lean teaches a style of management for after someone has taken initiative to create a project. *The Lean Startup* states: "Once a team is set up, what should it do? What process should it use? How should it be held accountable to performance milestones? These are questions the Lean Startup methodology is designed to answer."

Stanford's course description for The Lean LaunchPad: Getting Your Lean Startup off the Ground states (my emphasis): "Apply the Lean Startup principles including the Business Model Canvas, Customer Development, and Agile Engineering to prototype, test, and iterate on **your idea** while discovering if you have a profitable business model. This is the class adopted by the National Science Foundation and National Institutes of Health as the Innovation Corps. **Team applications required** in December."

Lean courses nearly always require you to apply and the applications ask you to describe your idea and team. Requiring an idea and a team is like saying, "To train a dog, start with a trained puppy."

That's the hard part!

Lean helps people whose interests led them to a potentially marketable idea—STEM types, maybe populous on campuses and Silicon Valley–type places, but small overall.

What about the rest of us?

What about people without great ideas or teams but who know they can develop them, who aren't scientists and engineers, and who don't know all that jargon but do know success doesn't require it?

What if you don't have an idea or even know how to create one? What if you don't know how to find anyone to join your team? What if you want to initiate a project but not start a company? Lean would not have helped Rafael or Jonathan. It may even have made starting projects seem less accessible.

Part of Lean's process is iterating ideas, so nearly everyone changes what they start with, which is nice, but the requirement increases the barrier to start, and you can't iterate what hasn't started.

I receive promotions from several departments at Columbia and NYU of entrepreneurship programs they run, as well as from city, state, and federal agencies. Nearly all of these programs are rooted in Lean methodology and culminate in a Dog Show spectacle. All require applicants to start with an idea and a team. Most focus on technological innovation and target STEM fields. Even those outside STEM, such as social entrepreneurship, still follow the Dog Show model.

Their funding generally comes from the Dog Show Cabal, motivated to pay back their investors and voters. Sponsors' interests may conflict with teaching you to take initiative, helping you do what you love, or helping you find and act on your passions.

I'll be the first to say that Lean helps many people in the communities it serves. Lean teaches how to engineer success, which is valuable for its audience. It changes the lives of people with ideas and teams, but it discourages others. Since the population of STEM fields is small compared to the full population, it's possible its net effect on entrepreneurship is negative if it discourages people outside STEM fields from starting.

Learning to take initiative is more fundamental and is prior to Lean, as Chris noted. Knowing how to initiate effectively may lead you to start companies where Lean would help. It may take you in other directions too.

Like Chris, people who have learned Method Initiative, Lean, and Design Thinking report that Method Initiative gives a human approach that the others don't, that it addresses *why* they act, what their work *means*, how to *connect* with people to *improve* their lives, and how to *grow* as people themselves.

Values

Lean and Design Thinking might have helped me build my first company, as a scientist who came up with an idea in a team. Building a company doesn't necessarily mean improving one's life, though. The management processes these methodologies develop don't start with your values. They'll lead a project to business success, but are neutral on your values and if those values match your project, they can lead you to succeed at something you don't like.

As much as I loved developing an idea I conceived of and the company I co-founded, like many STEM-originated ideas, my idea was a solution in search of a problem. The problem my idea solved turned out to be advertisers wanting to reach more people. My idea enabled us to offer a captive audience—great for advertisers, but inconsistent with my interests (which is why I also made art with it).

I didn't want a gravestone that said: "He brought ads to captive audiences." Lean may have made me externally successful but internally conflicted, which is why I wonder about Google's founders.

5

THE SOLUTION, PART 2
METHOD INITIATIVE

The dancer is realistic. His craft teaches him to be. Either the foot is pointed or it is not. No amount of dreaming will point it for you. This requires discipline, not drill, not something imposed from without, but discipline imposed by you yourself upon yourself.

Your goal is freedom. But freedom may only be achieved through discipline. In the studio you learn to conform, to submit yourself to the demands of your craft, so that you may finally be free.

MARTHA GRAHAM
visionary and revolutionary initiator in modern dance

IMAGINE IF ALL piano teachers taught by lecturing music theory in classrooms for hours at a time for years, assigning papers and case studies and giving tests on music theory. Only after years would students to put their fingers on a piano keyboard.

I suspect that few people would learn piano in that world. Those who did, perhaps coerced by our educational system, might not enjoy it. Those who excelled would probably leave the system to succeed on their own.

Imagine that in this world, someone started teaching piano how we teach it today—through playing scales, then simple exercises, then more challenging exercises, and so on to mastery. Once the "new" way took root, few would teach the old way again.

Playing piano is not academic. It's active, social, emotional, expressive, and performance-based (ASEEP). Taking initiative is ASEEP too. There are many such fields—acting, playing musical instruments, sports, dance, the military, singing, and so on. None do we teach mainly by lecture, case study, reading and writing papers, abstract analysis, or any standard technique of classroom learning. We teach them by starting with the basics and advancing. You start piano with scales. You start tennis with ground strokes. The military begins with basic training.

Basic doesn't mean *trivial* or *only for beginners*: masters still practice the basics too. LeBron James practices the same jump shots before the NBA finals and Serena Williams practices the same ground strokes before Wimbledon that a novice does. You never outgrow the basics. On the contrary, they lead to mastery, and the greatest masters practice them the most.

When I took salsa lessons, I asked my teachers how to lead fancy spins. To my annoyance, they told me to focus on my footwork and listen to the rhythm—the same lessons we started with and that I thought I'd moved past. You lead spins with your hands, right? On the contrary, I learned that when you move your feet to the rhythm, spins come easy. If you don't, they don't. Everything comes from the basics.

Magic happens when you practice the basics enough: you become fluent in the language of your craft. Though the basics you start with are mechanical, your voice emerges. Masters of ASEEP fields express themselves authentically and genuinely. That's why Kobe Bryant's words could lead to an Oscar for the animated short *Dear Basketball*.

Beginners tend to ask about advanced moves, as I did learning salsa, but they'll learn best through the basics. Beginners may fear that everyone focusing on the same basics will lead to conformity, but the opposite happens. Every performer develops his or her unique voice and style.

John McPhee, the Pulitzer Prize–winning author who wrote on personality in tennis in *Levels of the Game*, described how ASEEP fields bring out unique voices and styles: "A person's tennis game begins with his nature and background and comes out through his motor mechanisms into shot patterns and characteristics of play. If he is deliberate, he is a deliberate tennis player; and if he is flamboyant, his game probably is, too."

Initiative and entrepreneurship are fundamentally social and emotional, so the basics in our field are social and emotional skills. Emotional skills include awareness of your emotions and motivations, motivating yourself, and regulating your emotions. Social skills include reading others' emotions and motivations, influencing and motivating them, and making them feel understood. Learning them through practice will teach you faster and more thoroughly than reading about them or watching videos, no matter how prominent the writer, how cutting-edge the research, or how many views of the TED talk.

Primary roles of an instructor in such a field include developing effective exercises and motivating their practice. The instructor needs to know the theory—not to lecture, but to create effective exercises to reveal it through their practice. Passive observation doesn't teach performance, whether through lectures, books you only read, videos, or TED talks. That's why Part Two of this book gives you the basics of initiative for you to practice.

You've probably seen this image:

SUCCESS

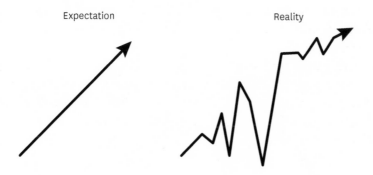

Expectation

Reality

The path on the right applies to most *projects*, but not to your *personal growth*. You may feel like you're on an emotional roller coaster and you will have many ups, downs, and unexpected turns, but the steps you take for your personal growth are straightforward. That's why we all start piano with scales and dance with footwork. Improv theater is spontaneous and unpredictable, but the exercises are well-established, as is the order to take them. My podcast interview[1] with Everett Spain, head of the U.S. Military Academy West Point's Department of Behavioral Science and Leadership, shows how the process to teach military leadership is methodical, tried, and true, as with most ASEEP fields. The exercises change between fields and get refined over time, but the straightforward steps are to practice, practice, practice. If you keep with it, you will develop as far as you want.

My last book, *Leadership Step by Step*, recognized that leadership was ASEEP too, and taught leadership by practicing exercises that started with the basics and advanced. I call this technique Method Learning and its result Method Leadership, based on the name that the field of acting uses, known as simply "the Method" or "Method Acting." *Leadership Step by Step*'s exercises dramatically change how the people who do them see and practice leadership, making it natural, easy, and fun.

| The emotional journey people expect and how it can feel. | What you actually do in Method Initiative. |

I call what this book teaches *Method Initiative*, with a specific application being Method Entrepreneurship, which I've taught in person and online to hundreds of people, embodied in the exercises in Part Two. The exercises are our equivalent of piano scales and basic training. For the rest of the book, for brevity, I'll write only Method Initiative, though everything applies equally to Method Entrepreneurship, which is a specific application.

Learning this way requires overcoming social and emotional challenges, as in all ASEEP fields. You may feel challenged in ways you weren't at school and work, but it's deeply rewarding and no harder or riskier than mainstream compliance-based learning.

Method Initiative skills apply to any field you might take initiative in, just as scales apply to most musical styles. If you start learning classical, after enough practice, you might find you prefer jazz and switch to it, then from jazz to improv theater. Some Method practitioners stick with one field for a majority of their lives, like Yo-Yo Ma or Meryl Streep (mostly), as you might. Others switch, like Steve Martin and Arnold Schwarzenegger, as you might.

Practice taking initiative enough and, before you know it, you'll love what you do and people will reward you for doing it. Your dream may evolve from the outside perspective, but you'll know you're becoming more true to you. In my case, I consider myself doing more science working on the environment than I did in the astrophysics lab, putting me in the lineage I always wanted to join of Aristotle, Galileo, Newton, Einstein, and Feynman, just by way of Rachel Carson, Dennis Meadows, and Donella Meadows.

You may feel anxious at first. Most beginners in ASEEP fields do. That's why the Method Initiative exercises start modestly and build simply. Steady progress, however modest, eventually develops you.

The route to your Carnegie Hall is through practicing exercises that work. Your passion and voice will emerge. You don't need an idea or team to start. They will emerge with practice. You'll wonder how you ever believed you needed them first. Mastery will come with practice. You'll feel ups and downs, but soon enough will find and live your passion, meaning, value, importance, and purpose beyond your horizons today. You will attract people who support you and whom you support back. People will thank you for your improving their lives. They'll reward you to keep you going, emotionally and materially.

You'll only wish you had started earlier.

GRACE

The first thing you notice about Grace is her dyed hair, which I've seen green, blue, red, and purple, and her dark clothes. On others this look might suggest campus radical, goth, or punk, but her quiet, unassuming manner suggests a librarian who goes out to concerts. I suspect no one would suggest when she took my class that she was a born entrepreneur or saleswoman, including herself.

Grace grew up outside Boston and attended NYU, where two New York City mainstays influenced her—music and inequality. She loved music and attended concerts, though she didn't get behind the scenes and take initiative. Likewise, the city's inequalities affected her too—homeless people living outside dorms housing college students paying six figures for an education many party through—but she didn't initiate there either. Like most college students, she went to school for a diploma and saw things outside school as distractions. Work was for after commencement, when she could commence life with a job with a manager to manage her—why else would it be called *commencement*? Besides, what difference could a student make?

With New York filled with music startups, she figured learning about entrepreneurship would help her get a job, which led her to my class. She anticipated a class in entrepreneurial appreciation, though she wouldn't have called it that, so when in the first session I explained that each student would create a project on a problem they cared about affecting people they cared about, and the steps they'd follow—the Method Initiative exercises in Part Two—she nearly dropped the class. She had no idea what to start a project on. She didn't come to school expecting to affect the lives of strangers. She just wanted someone to tell her what entrepreneurship was and tell her what to read so she could write a paper or take a test. Initiative was for other people.

Somehow she stayed. She simply followed the exercises. For her area of interest (exercise 1 on page 123), she chose music. As a problem in that area (exercise 2 on page 127), she chose the pain of high ticket prices for students, especially summer festivals. It was September and she had just shelled out hundreds of dollars for a couple of summer festivals.

The next exercises had her talk to people for advice (exercises 3 to 6). Those structured conversations led her to refine her ideas into a project. She knew some summer festivals had programs where some people—usually students—worked at the event instead of paying for tickets, picking up trash, giving directions, or other menial tasks. The exercises led her to come up with a rudimentary solution to her problem, which she refined into a project: for participants to earn their tickets working at soup kitchens, food pantries, and other places where they could help the disadvantaged instead of at the festival.

Everybody would benefit. The festival would gain favorable publicity more valuable than the menial labor it sacrificed. Participants would perform meaningful work. The places they worked would get free labor. Grace's role would be to work with city government to enroll the organizations, then with the organizations and volunteers to make sure they showed up and worked. The work being meaningful would make the publicity for the festival genuine.

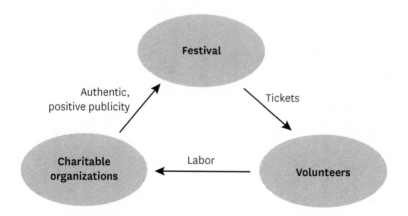

She felt anxious but did the exercises as assigned. By November, the exercises led her to work with people in the field (exercise 6). She found addresses for several festivals and cold emailed them.

Shortly before Thanksgiving, when I asked the class for updates, Grace read a response from a festival she loved, Governors Ball.

As she later recalled, "I reached out to them and after a few correspondences they basically told me, 'If you can come into our office by December 5 with a solid presentation, with a solid proposal, then this project is yours.'"

In other words, a job offer.

Having expected to start a job search a year later, to send out countless résumés, go to countless interviews, and work her way to a company of her dreams, Grace didn't know how to interpret their response.

She continued, "This was about mid-November. I told Josh that this is what they said to me and Josh said, 'This is a job offer' and it really blew me away. I started this class as someone totally scared of entrepreneurship and then, all of a sudden, I had this job offer on the table from Governors Ball."

She visited their offices, where a founder met her, telling her he liked her proposal.

She presented her plan to the team. They liked it.

By winter break, she started an internship as part of the GovBall team.

Over the break she started developing the project, called Governors Ball Gives Back (GBGB).

They launched GBGB in the spring. Volunteers filled the roughly 100 slots in days. Each worked 12 to 15 hours to attend the festival and meet labor regulations she'd had to research. The organizations welcomed their work.

Grace said about the experience, "One thing that was really striking for me from this program, probably the most meaningful moment, was after it was over, when I asked for feedback from the volunteers on what they thought. One girl emailed me back and said, 'I've never had the opportunity to do something like this before. I've never volunteered. I've never given my time like this and it was one of the most meaningful things I've ever done. I've already made plans to go back to these organizations and keep volunteering.'"

Grace continued, "Even if nothing else happened for me, even if it ended right there, I would have considered it a success. The whole point of creating this program for me was to use music festivals to kind of spark that kind of inspiration to bring to light these issues to people. And it all started with one very simple email that I sent to the info@govball.com account."

The results of her initiative continued. That summer, at 19 years old, she presented to Live Nation, a publicly traded company running festivals around the world. She later interned with them.

The next fall she spoke at Harvard about the project. *Forbes* profiled her.[2]

The next year, students in my class told me about friends of theirs participating in GBGB, not knowing a student in my earlier class created it.

On graduation, she took a job at the Richard Branson–funded music startup Sofar Sounds. Her experience made the hiring process easy. She loves her work.

6

THE MYTHS

IF I SEE anything that separates people who learn to take initiative from everyone else, a few myths do. People who don't learn believe them. Successful initiators believe their opposites, despite often believing them at first. Experience changed their beliefs. Similar myths haunt every ASEEP field. Practitioners in each make the same transition through practice, as will you.

Your biggest hurdles aren't external. External ones are a matter of using your skills, experiences, and beliefs.

Most people's biggest challenges are internal, usually beliefs justifying why they haven't acted. So many people believe and per-petuate the same beliefs that they become myths.

Some you need only overcome once. Others you have to over-come over and over. They help us sleep at night despite not realiz-ing our dreams. They give us palliative short-term peace of mind at the cost of our power to realize our dreams.

We begin to believe our stories after telling them enough.

Here are the top myths that keep us from initiating. I see them in my clients and students, in the media, and in Dog Show sources. I have held each of them and still find myself succumbing to them. I'll cover their antidotes in the next chapter.

The Myth of the Great Idea

The most common reason I hear for not starting a project is that people feel they need a great idea first. They see successful companies with successful projects and imagine they started that way.

They didn't. Pick any successful company or project. In nearly every case, its founding idea either didn't look promising at first or began as a different idea and evolved.

Google, for example, makes its money from advertising. In the '90s, its founders created search technology for portals, where they faced a saturated market dominated by Yahoo! Excite, AltaVista, and other incumbents. They tried to sell them their technology, dreaming of getting $1 million for it, but found no buyers. In other words, nobody believed they had even a million-dollar idea, let alone a multi-billion-dollar one.

Before Walmart, the big cities were dominated by Sears and its peers, who didn't care about smaller markets. Only after growing in the small-town markets the incumbents didn't care about did Walmart discover that in a modest-sized market, one Walmart could drive out existing small stores, create a local monopoly, and raise prices. Whatever its effects on American culture, the strategy that emerged was very profitable, but nobody saw it at first.

Consider Facebook's start. It had to take on Myspace. The prevailing wisdom said that network effects determined market success, and Myspace had hundreds of millions of users. Myspace also had Rupert Murdoch, an experienced media competitor, while a college undergraduate ran Facebook.

Twitter didn't begin as what we know it as now.

Nobody expected Grameen Bank to succeed. Yet it played a great role in establishing microlending and earned its founder, Muhammad Yunus, a Nobel Peace Prize.

Tesla followed decades of failed new American car ventures and failed electric car attempts.

Who believed boycotting buses in Montgomery, Alabama, could lead to federal civil rights legislation a decade later? Many considered nonviolent civil disobedience weak and ineffective.

Some women were the first to wear pants. Can you imagine the ridicule and scorn they faced? Yet few have influenced billions as they did. They continue to inspire me as people tell me my environmental activities will amount to nothing. Their living by their values helps me live by mine. That's initiative.

The list of successes that emerged from questionable ideas goes on. The more you look at any project—business or otherwise—the more you'll find it began not with surety and confidence but with people iterating and persisting—not blindly or bullheadedly, but through simple techniques, such as those Method Initiative teaches.

The Myth of the Great Résumé

The second most common answer people give me for not starting projects is that they want to build their résumé. I particularly hear this reason from students, especially in top institutions.

Since few things help more than experience, they have a point. Older founders succeed more than younger, despite the media's preoccupation with founders in their 20s. Industry connections help too.

But no one buys a product or service because of the seller's résumé. They buy or support your cause because you offer something they expect will improve their lives more than it costs.

Not all experience helps equally. Corporate experience doesn't necessarily translate to success taking initiative. As we've seen, many employees and students at top institutions excel at following and complying. Our culture promotes filling résumés and transcripts with double majors, triple minors, and so on—but not finishing what you started.

You know who succeeds more than older founders? Previous founders. The distinction is between *any* experience and *relevant* experience.

You know what kind of experience helps you succeed at taking initiative? *Taking initiative!*

The best way to develop the skills to initiate is to initiate. You don't have to try to create the next Google, but starting something, however modest, will teach you more than following others. Even if you want to win Best in Show, the best way is still Method Initiative.

RJ

RJ is saving lives with his project and changing culture. While still in college, he delivered a riveting, inspirational TEDx talk on his project, and the Dalai Lama named him a Dalai Lama fellow.

Like Grace, before Method Initiative RJ didn't know he would create a project affecting people he cared about beyond the school walls. He didn't have an idea to start with. He was thinking about dropping out. In his words, "Coming into that sophomore year I was all over the place. I didn't know my purpose. I didn't know if I belonged at NYU. I said, 'Oh, maybe I should go back home.' I was really looking for a sense of purpose in New York and then in my college career."

Instead, he uncovered a deep passion and a project based on it. Soon he was leading teams including professionals with advanced degrees, equally impassioned.

RJ is a Palestinian American born and raised in Las Vegas. He grew up with some sense of his ancestral heritage and spoke Arabic, but didn't focus on it. By sophomore year he had interned on Capitol Hill and worked with NYU's Muslim Student Association.

He didn't have a great idea.

He describes starting the exercises like this: "When I was in the class it started off as big grand idea of going to rebuild the Gaza Strip. I remember it was called the Gaza Strip Redevelopment Plan, and one of the things that you taught us in class that I still think about almost every day is, 'Better than a great idea is an okay idea with market feedback and iterations.'"

How did he turn his naive idea into a globally recognized project while in his teens? I wish I could tell a dramatic story of epiphany and a hero's journey, but he just did the exercises. They don't look exciting from the outside, but, as in any Method Field, doing them will lead you to find in yourself more passion, discovery, and growth than with any other way.

In a reflection on developing the project, RJ wrote, "I've taken [my original plan] to transition it from what was an idea of living in the Gaza Strip for two years to rebuild it to being in a refugee camp in the West Bank called New Askar, where there's a 70-percent unemployment rate and high drug abuse and no police presence, to creating a four-week-long summer leadership camp for youth in that refugee camp. We hope to implement it next summer."

He has since created LEAD Palestine, an organization that teaches effective leadership skills to Palestinian youths in the West Bank. RJ's TEDx talk and the project's website, leadpalestine.com, explain the project in more depth, but briefly, he and his team are teaching Palestinian youths leadership skills—not command-and-control authoritarian practice, but self-awareness, listening, creating meaning and value for others, teamwork, and so on (based in part on Method Leadership from my book and my course, *Leadership Step by Step*).

Beyond giving hope to the youths he serves, RJ is leading them to act in new ways. He's helping them develop self-awareness, express themselves, learn to achieve results without violence, organize effectively, question reactive practices that can turn violent, and more. Older Palestinians report that LEAD Palestine is bringing a new and effective style of leadership and education to the community.

The youths RJ serves inspire him back. His TEDx talk, for example, describes[1] how his program transformed one young man so despondent and hopeless that he aspired to martyr himself with a suicide bomb. LEAD Palestine led the young man to find hope and goals in sport—soccer, especially. At the time of RJ's TEDx talk, that student was playing for the National Youth League of Palestine, soon to represent Palestine in a competition in Manchester, England. He chose to spread understanding and sport.

Will RJ succeed in the long term? We can't say yet, but he's influenced many people in ways they, their families, and their communities thank him for. Beyond what comes of LEAD Palestine, RJ will keep succeeding. He loves what he's doing. He's creating value. Everyone involved in his project loves their work.

If you think projects need great ideas, few seem less practical than a college student in New York rebuilding the Gaza Strip. If you're concerned you're lacking ideas, I hope his success despite starting with an idea so unactionable and naive, at least in my opinion, bolsters your confidence.

The Myth of the Born Entrepreneur/ Leader/Salesperson

What sells movie tickets and ad space? Superheroes, fantasy, and drama.

What doesn't? Consistent, methodical work.

However undramatic from the outside, passion-driven, consistent, methodical work is as rewarding as it gets. It gets results.

It's relieving to tell ourselves that someone who succeeded where we didn't had advantages we don't. But a belief making you feel good doesn't make it accurate.

Nobody was born selling, leading, or even talking. Every successful behavior you see was learned through practice. What they can learn, you can too. If you haven't yet, that doesn't mean you can't.

I'm not saying it's easy to learn what they did, but it wasn't easy for them either.

I'm also not saying that people aren't born with family connections or wealth. Children of billionaires will have access to material resources and connections others don't. You can still initiate and solve problems in communities you care about. No one has greater access to happiness, satisfaction, and emotional reward.

Method Initiative doesn't enable you to solve *any* problem for *anyone*, but no matter your station in life, you can solve problems you care about for people you care about so that they support you. Solving problems and building community improves it.

It's possible that being the best in the world at something requires some accident of birth. You won't likely become the best basketball player if you're five feet tall or 50 years old. But success at taking initiative doesn't require being the best in the world. What *can* you do? What problems *can* you solve? You aren't restricted to one area to act. As you'll find as you practice the exercises, you can apply the techniques in many areas.

The Myth of the Great Elevator Pitch

Many aspiring entrepreneurs work on developing elevator pitches— perfect project descriptions short enough to lead a dream contact trapped in a brief elevator ride with you to want to meet again. While nothing is wrong with short, effective descriptions, rarely will you find important people trapped with you, in elevators or anyplace else. The concept of elevator pitches comes from and reinforces a feeling of scarcity. Meanwhile, since there is no end to improving them, founders spend inordinate amounts of time on them that they could spend on developing their projects. Many people with great elevator pitches can't back them up when grilled afterward, since practicing the pitch distracted from the basics.

The best way to create effective, short descriptions is to present repeatedly, each time iterating, developing what works, eliminating what doesn't. Presenting often comes from a place of abundance. It also leads you to learn to handle many questions and responses. Method Initiative creates many supportive relationships, which enable many presentations. It also leads you to create meaningful relationships with valuable people so you don't have to rely on hope and contrivances. Method Initiative teaches you how to meet people, however valuable, confidently, so they want to listen to and support you.

In other words, the most effective way to achieve the results of a great elevator pitch is not to build the pitch itself but instead to build a project you love, creating relationships along the way, presenting often—that is, by practicing Method Initiative. You'll progress faster and see focusing on elevator pitches as distracting.

The Myth of Needing Resources

Many people think you need money, free time, connections, or other resources to start a successful project. Rafael thought so at first.

On the contrary, few social problems get solved by one person alone. Solutions come from teams, with different members contributing what one person can't.

You've heard it's not what you know but whom you know. Likewise, it's not what resources you have, but knowing who has them and how to motivate them to grant you access. And beyond whom you know are the skills to create relationships, which will get you the whom and what. Method Initiative develops the social and emotional skills to approach and create supportive relationships with people with access to resources. Rafael stopped believing he didn't have the resources to start projects and started making accessing those resources early steps of the project.

MARCO

Marco is a graphic designer born in Mexico City, where he attended college. He told me, "I moved to New York in 2012 with all my savings [about $1,000] and after some struggle I landed a job at an advertising startup; that has led me to develop a career around digital advertising, and lately a lot of UX/UI as I'm learning to code." He took my course a few years later.

Before Method Initiative, he believed that "to be an entrepreneur you needed to have capital beforehand . . . money or acquaintances who were in the kind of business you were pursuing."

After his project in our class, he told me, "I learned a whole new level of interpersonal relationships; I learned a lot about business, setting up online processes, and effective marketing... next time it will be considerably easier."

He added, "I think it only takes initiative and hard work to make an entrepreneur; money doesn't come in the mix... Anyone with a deep enough interest and a strong enough will to make things happen surely can."

I can't wait to see his next project.

As Marco learned, when you've mastered these skills, needing resources only means adding the steps to your project of using the skills to meet people with access to the resources and involving them in the project.

The Myth of Needing a Passion

Some people say, "Forget about not having a great idea. I don't even have direction. I don't have the passion to start a project."

Everyone's situation is unique, but the most common reason I see for believing you don't care about anything is to protect yourself from judgment and vulnerability. If you don't believe you care about anything then you can't try and risk failing.

Many of us have hidden our cares and passions for so long we forgot we were hiding them. Reading this book, however, means something is motivating you. You care about something.

Caring about something and doing some things and not others means you care about some things more than others. The greatest passions of people who think they lack them tend to be what they protect most, and are therefore hard for beginners to sense. You'll easily sense generic interests like music, movies, books, and travel that everyone shares but that don't expose your vulnerabilities.

Passions become obvious when you find them, often with feelings of epiphany when you see they've been there for a long time.

How do you find latent or suppressed passions? Ineffective ways include sitting and introspecting, thinking, analyzing, answering questionnaires, or talking things through—unless you're talking to someone who knows what to ask.

What works is acting on what you have access to, however tepid it may feel, forcing yourself to choose among competing options and values, and developing the skills, experiences, and beliefs of taking initiative. The more you develop them, the greater you will expect success in future endeavors. The more you expect to succeed, the more sensitive you'll become to other latent passions.

You'll also lose patience for tepid things. Initiating projects on once-suppressed passions will lead you to seek out more of them. You'll keep discovering them. You'll see that the signs of your suppressed passions were always there, you just looked past them to protect your vulnerabilities. You'll view your former self as having been incomplete, maybe fake.

You'll only wish you had started earlier.

The Myth of Too Many Passions
(aka Fear of Missing Out, aka Fear of Regret)

Many people feel they have too many passions and can't choose between them. They're afraid that picking the wrong one will divert them from their true passion, which they'll miss out on and regret. On the contrary, the most effective way to find and act on your greatest passion is to act on any interest you sense might have potential, develop the Method skills, and apply them to your next interest. I'll expand on this strategy and why it works in chapter 8.

Many people continue with several at once, seeing themselves as indecisive when feeling bad or a Renaissance man or woman when feeling good. What worked for Leonardo may work for them, but more often this route leads to mediocrity in many areas, mastery in none. You have to say no to a lot of good things to have a great life.

Muddling along with several, they hope a big break in one will help them choose. But big breaks rarely happen by chance, however lucky they appear from the outside. They result from initiative.

Method Initiative leads people to wish they had picked one and dropped the rest earlier. Looking back, they see that they didn't value their various interests equally. They lacked the skill to sense their priorities and act on them, leading to indecision.

Developing that skill and experience led me to create one of Method Initiative's most valuable parts—switching projects. Switching teaches you to sense different levels of passion and to develop more meaningful ones. It emerged from students who switched consistently finding that they preferred their new projects. I created a rule that they could switch projects at any stage but would have to restart from step one. While restarting might sound onerous, experience showed the opposite. Students who switched found that redoing the exercises revealed that they had learned more than they thought, giving them confidence. Repeating even eight or nine out of ten exercises that first took a week each would take as little as a week in total the second time through.

More importantly, they valued the new projects more, having chosen them based on greater experience. Their appreciation went beyond the projects themselves. They discovered latent passions they hadn't previously allowed themselves to sense or act on. They saw their old projects not as distractions or red herrings but as essential steps to learn about themselves, their relationships, their fears, their dreams, and more. They looked back on their old projects with gratitude.

I had tried before that rule to figure out a way to help people avoid switching, which I now see as misguided. We learn from experience. Bypassing experience deprived them of learning how to discover their passions. The goal of Method Initiative is only partly to help you create a particular project. The greater, long-term goal is to teach you to create projects in general.

ESTHER

Esther took my class as a senior, not knowing she'd start a project. Little did she know the effect the class would have on her education and career. Little did I know that I would learn as much from her.

Through most of the class she did solid work. She had traveled the summer before and chose to develop an app to help travelers.

Before week 8, she asked to meet for office hours.

She said, "I like your class and how it's experiential and we're working on real life. The thing is, I'm planning on going to law school, so I want to make sure I get an A."

Wondering, based on her focus on the credential, if she got the point of the course, I commented how much more enthusiastic she sounded about law than she did about her travel app, and asked her to elaborate.

She told me that she wanted to learn law to apply it to social work, which she cared more about.

I said, "Going to law school for social work means you'll take a long time to pay for it. You must love social work."

Her eyes lit up and she began to speak about social work with an animation that was night and day compared to her talk about the travel app. She described the value social workers created, but how society didn't value their contributions, a situation which she felt a calling to change.

I asked why she didn't choose something in social work for her project.

She gave a few cursory reasons—she didn't think a project in social work would make much money, no one else was doing anything like it, and she wasn't sure it would work.

I'd heard similar reasons from students before. They told me on reflection that they chose projects to do what they thought they were supposed to, or that were "appropriate" for school, not caring for them.

I said, "You could get an A with the travel app, but I see how much more you care about social work and law. Switching projects would mean you would have to work more and may temporarily make you feel like you're going backward, but you would enjoy doing it more and you'd benefit a lot more."

I reminded her how fast students caught up and how much more they learned after switching, then continued, "Here's the big benefit. Since you're solving problems you care about for a community you care about, it's fine with me if your project helps you personally. If you create a law and social work project, you can use the exercises to talk to people in your field, like professors at law schools you want to apply to. Professors who would never respond to you asking for help getting into the school will answer your call about a project to help people that they care about too."

She started to see how she could *actually* work on something she *actually* cared about and *actually* make a difference.

"It may sound Machiavellian, but few things help an application more than a recommendation from a professor at the school you're applying to. It's not self-serving, though, when your project helps a community you and they care about," I continued. "You might also find you don't like law or social work since you only know the fields from the outside. If you aren't going to like it, it's probably better to find out now than with six figures of debt and years of your life spent. Or you might find you can achieve your goals without law school."

Esther told me that she did have an idea of a social work project—in fact, from before class started (a common pattern).

As the office hour ended, she faced the choice between the old project and the rediscovered one. I told her she didn't have to decide then and there.

At our next class she had done the homework for the travel app, but told me she was thinking more about the new project. By the last class she had switched and caught up. In the later exercises, she reached out and spoke to law school professors, creating meaningful relationships with them.

Ultimately, she got into a top law school. Before starting it, she said about the exercises, "I thought I knew how to do school already. I knew what to do. I knew how to take a test and write a paper. What are these assignments, like cold calling people, iterating my ideas? I never did that."

She continued, "I didn't get it initially but I was happy with the experience because it gave me skills I needed as opposed to my other courses, where I wrote papers and took tests. I wasn't just memorizing information, I was learning on the go. Now I find it more valuable than I even realized at the time. Like knowing how to contact people and not being afraid to reach out, not feeling awkward, knowing what to say, knowing how to structure an email. It challenged me on a personal level and gave me the confidence to say, 'I *do* have good ideas and they *are* worth sharing. People will appreciate them.' Even if people I approach don't appreciate them now, others will."

Esther told me recently, "I'm about to start my second year at law school and I've learned much more out of the classroom than my classmates. When I'm curious about a new field or company, I call or email the professor or someone at the firm. Then I do something with them to find out if I want to do more or not. And many things I don't like, but that's how I find out. As much as I loved social work, I had no idea how much more there was to law, so I'm trying many other things."

She continued, "My classmates ask how I get internships and to work with professors and organizations like the Innocence Project. I tell them I just call and ask. Since no one else does, I get the chances. They just go to class and wait for things to happen." And Method Initiative, she explains, is "where I learned to find out about things by talking to people and doing them."

As much as Esther learned from the class, I learned as much from our office hour. Until then, I had struggled to help students find the right project for them from the start, to help them avoid redoing exercises and wasting time on projects they didn't care about.

Her experience clarified what I should have seen from the start, knowing how much more people learn by doing than by following.

Starting projects means you can never be sure they will be worth your time or if you'll like others more. The skills involved in choosing an idea, developing it, and finding what you care about come through experience. Traditional education tells you, "Here's what's important, do it," and robs you of your chance to learn what *you* consider important. You may learn about values in the abstract, but you don't learn what you care about and what you value. School today atrophies these skills.

Trying to solve problems for them further robs them of developing the skills to develop ideas they care about. Method Initiative makes you increasingly sensitive to how you feel about things, so you find passions and values you didn't sense before. You become confident in your ability to make them work or drop them if they don't, knowing you can find a new problem, which enables you to share, develop, iterate, and act on them with confidence and enthusiasm.

The Sources of the Myths:
What Method Initiative Overcomes

The myths I just listed feed on our need to protect ourselves. They come from many sources, but the main ones I see are ignorance, vulnerability and fear of judgment, and insecurity.

Ignorance

Nobody believes that dog shows represent the only way to raise a dog, but many people believe that Dog Show Entrepreneurship represents entrepreneurship. They believe entrepreneurship has to follow steps like getting funding, developing an elevator pitch, and so on.

Starting ventures is only one way to take initiative—a tiny subset. Jackie Robinson took initiative, but not to start a company. So did the students and clients in this book, and so did I with my podcast and writing.

The more you practice Method Initiative, the more opportunities you will see and the more successful you will become at acting on them.

Vulnerability and fear of judgment

If no one knows what you care about, then their judgment doesn't hurt, because it isn't about you.

We were all teased as children. If kids tease you about something you can change, you change it. For things we care about, that are integral parts of us, that we can't or won't change, we often protect ourselves by hiding them.

As we grew, people used us, manipulated us, and fell out of love with us. Casual friends can't break our hearts. People we care about can. Caring makes us vulnerable. But protecting our vulnerabilities comes at the cost of enjoying what we care about.

Taking initiative exposes your cares and therefore your vulnerabilities. Many students and clients first choose projects they care little about, I suspect partly to protect themselves. I think many forgot what they cared about after decades of protection. They choose projects for impersonal reasons, like money, trends, parental pressure, and peer pressure.

By choosing for you, compliance-based education protects you from acting on your interests and therefore your vulnerabilities, but robs you of learning how. We all value family, community, health, and so on. The challenge in knowing your values is knowing which you care about more when they conflict. The challenge when you feel too many interests competing for your resources isn't determining which you like. It's which among the ones you like to get rid of. The -cide in decide means "cut off" or "kill," as in pesticide. The challenge is deciding which interest you're willing to cut off or kill.

Analysis and planning won't tell you. Only acting on your values will reveal the deepest ones. Method Initiative will help you discover them so you will feel confident acting on them.

Insecurity

Nobody values everything the same as you, not even (or especially not) your parents or spouse. Many people intending to help you and believing they are helping you will mislead you. Parents often promote stability. A spouse may want you to make more money. Teachers encourage you to do what you got an A in.

Learning your values and acting on them can reveal great discrepancies between what you care about and how you act—that is, between your values and your behavior. Many people choose comfort and convenience despite saying they value the challenge of growth. Some live their whole lives never becoming aware of the difference, let alone resolving it.

Method Initiative will reveal values you aren't acting on and enable you to act on them.

ANDREAS

Andreas came to me as a co-founder of a software company he wrote the code for. He's Swedish, living in Sweden, and we've never met in person.

The other co-founder and the company's main investor had offered to buy him out. He came to me for business coaching since he'd never created a deal for himself with such big numbers. It took time and new skills, but they came to a mutually satisfactory deal.

The deal meant that he wouldn't have to earn money for several years and that he had credibility from creating a business profitable enough for him to cash out—in other words, he had freedom to do what he wanted.

His path soon diverged from traditional entrepreneurship. Ironically, that alternate path led him to what on the outside looks less entrepreneurial, or even professional. But, in his words, "When I helped run that company, I saw business grow and I had to keep writing the software, so I felt like I must be on the right path. But my heart wasn't in it, even though I helped start it. I never asked what I wanted to do. I was doing what I thought I was supposed to and everyone congratulated me for it."

He continued, "I know that what I'm doing now looks from the outside like a step in an unusual direction, but I have more freedom than ever. I love what I do. I get more responsibilities when I want them. Entrepreneurship and initiative for me don't mean doing what everyone else does. They mean doing what I want to on my terms. I love what I'm doing."

What was his path and what does he do now?

First, he traveled, an interest he exhausted in six months. After that, he didn't want to found another company but he did want to work in an entrepreneurial environment. Since Method Initiative develops relationships with valuable people and presents you as a problem solver and initiator, it tends to lead to job offers, so we worked on it.

Soon he began working on a project of his creation. His relationships and network grew. He transformed from a programmer who follows to a problem solver who initiates. As his skills to meet and meaningfully connect with people grew, he organized a panel discussion of experts in his field.

He said, "Before starting the exercises I didn't think I had the confidence or skills to talk to people. I wouldn't expect them to see value in talking to me. Instead, I started talking with founders and CEOs who told me they needed people like me. As you mentioned, they were offering me jobs."

His new social and emotional skills were creating the what and whom he knew.

He continued, "The first guy that offered me a job, I thought, 'This is amazing!' I wanted to take it and I visited them a few times. But I could feel my skills developing week by week. By the time he formalized the offer, the panel was forming and I was meeting people at more prestigious places. These professional consulting firms invited me to interview and I realized I was beyond what that first place offered, even though at first I had felt lucky to talk to them."

He kept meeting people at places he felt more attracted to. Then everything changed. He said, "I realized that I felt grateful to all those places out of insecurity. I felt lucky to get any attention because I didn't feel confident in myself. As my skills increased, I realized I could do whatever I wanted if I set myself to it."

Each distraction dispensed with increased his confidence in taking new interests. The Myth of Too Many Passions would tell him not to act but instead to analyze before acting. Action leads to understanding and epiphany more than the other way around.

"Only then could I realize what I loved," said Andreas. "As much as I cared about entrepreneurship as everyone else defined it, I wanted to explore life and myself. Now that I could meet people and connect on passions, I wanted to apply these things everywhere in life. That's when I decided to move to Stockholm despite having no plans. I was no longer a programmer looking for work. I was an entrepreneur in the sense of creating the outcome I wanted. I was still doing the exercises, but my way, since I had internalized them."

Now, in Stockholm, amid the abundance of offers he's received, he chose two part-time jobs most people wouldn't take but that he loves. Three days a week he is a bike messenger and two days a week he canvasses for a non-profit he cares about.

Wait, what? Aren't those jobs taken by people without better options or training?

"Josh," he said, "I know how it looks, but I would pay to do what I do. I spent too long at a desk. Now I love working with people, getting in the best shape of my life. My time is mine. I got promoted to team leader as a messenger right away. My delivery times keep getting faster as I get in better shape. And some days canvassing, when I'm on, I bring in the most donations and the people who donate tell me they feel grateful to me. I feel like a great performer getting standing ovations."

Andreas may love these jobs for the rest of his life. Alternatively, he may learn all he can from them, exhaust them, and move on to things he loves more.

As I see it, he's getting paid to get intensive experiential training in leadership and sales while getting more fit. I predict this will result in him initiating a new project he loves that combines everything he's done so far.

Do I suggest everyone or even anyone should become a bike messenger and non-profit canvasser? Of course not, but I do recommend you exhaust your insecurities about lacking the skills, experiences, and beliefs to initiate and create what outcomes you want. I recommend you explore your passions based on thoughtful, reflective action, which Method Initiative provides, not by blindly doing what society values. I recommend you consider that accepting and acting on others' values can be a greater life risk than discovering and acting on your own.

As an update as this book goes to print, Andreas has taken a new job with a tech company. They are growing and he is employee number ten, depending on how you count. He works directly with the CEO/founder. He likes the stability and support of the company culture, which for him is new.

"It's important for me to go back to working in tech, in a small company, like my old company, but it's nice to get support from others instead of having to provide it myself. I believe in the company's culture and like the people. It's giving me opportunities—to learn, to earn money, and to grow both within the company and as an individual. I've already created my own projects based on the exercises we did together. I suggested one to the CEO, just like in our exercises, and he gave me the project and resources to implement it, including people's time. It feels great to have a project, especially so soon, that helps my coworkers."

Now, says Andreas, "when people talk about their problems, I think of more projects to help solve them."

3 ANTIDOTES AND
7 PRINCIPLES

I CAN TELL you the myths aren't true all day, but ultimately unlearning them comes from experiences that contradict them. Method Initiative works because it is based on three practices that give you those experiences.

3 Antidotes

1. Start with what you have access to

If you aren't sure of an interest to act on—you feel you have too few options or too many—apply the exercises on what you can. If you want to play a sport but aren't sure which, Method Initiative exercises are like cardiovascular and balance exercises. They will help in any direction you later choose. They're simple enough for beginners, and masters still use them.

2. Practice effective exercises

Why do athletes in many sports that don't involve weights or sprints lift weights and run sprints?

Because these exercises work. They build broadly useful skills and abilities.

While some people succeed just taking life as it comes, many more hit obstacles bigger than they can handle too early, and so learn helplessness. Tennis instructors don't start by teaching the serve, even though the game begins with it. You build up to advanced parts by starting with the basics. This book's exercises have been tested and refined with hundreds of cases. Are they the only way to learn to take initiative? No, but they work.

3. Take small steps

Anxiety comes from big steps. Nobody jumps from playing their first scales to playing Carnegie Hall in one step. Thinking about big dreams can scare many people. The way to Carnegie Hall without great anxiety is through small steps. The early Method Initiative exercises are simple enough for anyone. The advanced ones might challenge even seasoned initiators, but since each builds on the ones before and leads in small steps to the next, you won't have to make any big anxiety-causing jumps.

Some people want to create the next Google or disrupt an industry. Even if you do, your best path there is still Method Initiative. There's no conflict between loving your project and striking it rich—on the contrary, loving your project makes success more likely. You'll be surprised how quickly you develop.

If you want a dog to compete for Best in Show, the best thing you can do is learn to find a dog you love and care for it so it loves you back. Even if that dog never wins Best in Show, you and your dog will love each other and you'll learn to love dogs more in general.

7 Principles

Signposts and milestones help on a journey. They tell you that you're on the path, how far you've come, and where to go next.

The seven principles that follow will probably make some sense your first time reading them, but doing the exercises will imbue them with their full meaning and value. That growing meaning will tell you that you're developing the skills, experiences, and beliefs of effectively taking initiative.

1. Personality matters less than skills you can learn

This principle counters the disempowering and discouraging myth that leaders, entrepreneurs, and others who take initiative are born with something special.

The available evidence from exemplary social entrepreneurs suggests that success depends less upon personality than it does on teachable skills, such as the ability to activate the public, raise capital, negotiate results, and manage the difficult transitions involved in taking an organization from its initial start-up phase to maturity.[1]

PAUL C. LIGHT NYU Wagner School of Public Service

The media often present successful initiators and entrepreneurs as different and superior—smarter, more creative, more charismatic, more driven, and so on. Such portrayals sell magazines and movie tickets but aren't accurate or helpful.

Projects succeed not because of traits their founders were born with but because of skills they practice—and not just any skills, but skills you can learn.

As you develop skills, experiences, and beliefs from the exercises, you will find your effectiveness and interest growing. You'll find that the most meaningful measures of success are in the act of starting and in how well you reach your potential, not accidents of birth.

Beyond merely reaching your potential, you'll also measure your success by how much you increase that potential.

2. The idea of a lifetime comes once a month

People who don't know that great ideas emerge from a process, not a muse, alignment of stars, or outside source, see others' great ideas and think, "If only I got so lucky, I'd start something too."

Believing that a great idea is rare leads people to hold their ideas tightly and fear changing or losing them. They act out of scarcity, insecurity, and desperation.

Method Initiative makes creating projects increasingly easy. After doing the first few exercises a few times, you'll find you can turn problems into projects you love, usually spending little time and often no money. You'll know how to share these projects with valuable people who can help make them happen, leading them to support you.

Your problem will become filtering the great ideas from the merely good ones, and, even then, deciding among many. You'll act with confidence and generosity.

3. Better than a great idea is an okay idea plus market feedback, flexibility, and iterations

This principle counters the Myth of the Great Idea. RJ and Esther alluded to it.

We've covered that ideas rarely start successful. They start modestly. Method Initiative will teach you to turn even rudimentary ideas into great ones (or decide against ones that don't work). You'll learn the tools to do it: listening to people you want to serve, flexibility to allow your idea to evolve, and iterations.

The more you develop your skills to create modest ideas and evolve them into effective ones, the more sensitive you'll become to problems with the potential for greatness. Hence, you'll have plenty of ideas that could become the project of a lifetime.

The most useful measure of the quality of an idea is how many times you've iterated it based on advice from the market.

4. Start where you are with what you have

This principle counters thinking you have no ideas or too many.

If you have too many and fear regretting a choice, you will learn that, after eliminating those you know you don't want, choosing any one—not two or more but one—will either lead you to love it or become the most effective path to finding another that you love more. Like Esther, you'll bring yourself up to speed on the next one faster than you'd expect.

If you think you have no ideas, choosing anything you have access to will still help you most. You'll find that practicing Method Initiative exercises will develop your skills, experiences, and beliefs in initiating, which will increase your expectation of success, which will motivate you. They will increase your sensitivity to latent ideas.

5. Pitch and they'll judge. Ask advice and they'll help

People who believe ideas are the core of initiative want others to see their ideas' greatness. They pitch them not realizing that doing so leads the other person to judge them—a dynamic that tends to separate them. Evaluators who feel themselves on pedestals will often ask presenters to prove themselves—to coif and trot jauntily for them.

Pitching is the core of Dog Show Entrepreneurship. The Dog Show Cabal loves when initiators pitch. Trotting jauntily gets them ratings and makes you dependent. They can pick their favorites. They can support the project but not you.

Believing you need to start from an idea also leads people to push their ideas on everyone—called working in the *solution space*—even when listening instead of pushing could show you how to change your idea to solve the problem more effectively—called working in the *problem space*. We've all had someone try to fix something we didn't want fixed. They want thanks, we feel annoyed. We've done it too. It results from focusing on solutions over people feeling the problem. Problem space involves emotions, listening, and putting others first. If you're used to working in the solution space, switching can feel hard or misguided. You'll be amazed at the feeling of liberation, though, when people start telling you how to solve their problems and that they'll reward you for it.

Method Initiative leads you to create effective relationships with people in your field, ultimately with experts. Their feedback, combined with flexibility and iterations, will turn your modest ideas into great ones.

Asking advice creates relationships in which others see themselves in your project, leading them to support you. Think of times you gave people advice. Did you not feel something like, "Now when they succeed, it will be partly from my advice"? Didn't that thought make you feel vested in their success, motivating you to help them more?

In other words, Method Initiative leads you to create a supportive community with a vested interest in your success. You will attract mentors, teachers, and partners. You will emerge with the ability to create such relationships for the rest of your life.

6. The problem leads to the solution

Einstein supposedly answered the question "If you had one hour to save the world, how would you spend it?" with: "I would spend 55 minutes defining the problem and then five minutes solving it. The formulation of a problem is often more essential than its solution, which may be merely a matter of mathematical or experimental skill."

Aspiring initiators and entrepreneurs often try to improve their projects through focusing on the solution. Often, the more intelligent, smart, and clever the initiator, the deeper this affliction and the longer and harder they work on the solution, trying to hammer square pegs into round holes.

Our compliance-based educational system gave us decades of textbook problems whose solution came from brute force work. Life doesn't give us word problems.

The Dog Show Cabal's focus on pitches doesn't help. Nor does the common "Oh really, what's your idea?" response when people hear you're working on a project.

Method Initiative will teach you that focusing on understanding the problem will lead to its solution more effectively than any other technique. You'll feel natural learning people's problems in order to solve them.

The clearest sign of progress I see in students learning to initiate is their transition from focusing on the solution and how to show theirs off to focusing on the problem and the people feeling it. Beyond leading to more than effective solutions, it generates passion and inspires. Work becomes meaningful—a mission in service of others. It turns aimless interest into focused drive—a calling.

7. Almost nothing inspires like helping others so much that they reward you for it

"Reward" doesn't necessarily mean money, though it is important to most projects.

When you love your project, it's easy to fool yourself into thinking you're helping when you aren't. People don't buy your product because *you* think it can solve their problems. They buy it because *they* think it can. When you do your job well, they support you because they expect you will help them more than what they spend supporting you.

Many people confuse feeling good when people thank them with vanity or insecurity. On the contrary, that reciprocation means you're improving their lives by their values. I can't prove it, but I believe that as a social species we evolved to feel reward from others telling us we helped them. Whatever the reason, being recognized for our efforts feels incredibly rewarding.

There are two types of inspiration. One I call New Year's resolutions. People feel inspired to get more fit on December 31. Gyms are full in early January. Most people lose their inspiration by Valentine's Day. Self-serving inspirations tend to fade. That's not the inspiration that Method Initiative instills.

The other focuses on others and helping them. Think of a teacher who inspires students to work harder for a particular class, or Martin Luther King Jr. inspiring people to go to jail to create freedom for others. Inspiration to serve others can last a lifetime. Projects that align with your values and serve others create this second type of inspiration. "To serve is to live," in the words of Frances Hesselbein, the Presidential Medal of Freedom honoree and former CEO of the Girl Scouts whom Peter Drucker named "the best leader in America." Method Initiative creates this inspiration.

The Results

The short-term result of these exercises may be a project that realizes and fulfills your greatest passion, bringing you money, power, and fame. Such results fade, even if you become a titan of industry, a darling of Wall Street, or a celebrity. They pale in comparison to the enduring results of knowing how to identify and develop passions, not just in one project but everywhere—your professional life, with friends, family and loved ones, and internally.

You will live a life of passion, helping others so much that they reward you for it.

An anonymous review by one of my students said, "I expected this class to be worksheets and tests; instead I found phone calls and discussions. I found myself falling in love with my project and in love with being an entrepreneur. Passion for the project is what motivated me. I didn't want to go the extra mile to get a good grade, I wanted to go the extra mile because it was fun to work on the project and see my business plan become more and more concrete. My fellow classmates' passion about their projects drove them as well and we were all able to grow as entrepreneurs. I have never met people so excited by spreadsheets or frustrated by not being able to contact CEOs. This shared passion and excitement has made learning about entrepreneurship even more special."

8

INITIATIVE, ACTION, AND PASSION

SETH GODIN DESCRIBED[1] a pattern that successful people recognize:

> More than 400 published books. How did [Isaac] Asimov possibly pull this off?
>
> Asimov woke up every morning, sat in front of his manual typewriter, and he typed.
>
> That was his job, to type.
>
> The stories were the bonus that came along for the ride.
>
> He typed when he wasn't inspired. The typing turned into writing and he became inspired.
>
> We don't write because we feel like it.
>
> We feel like it because we write.
>
> **You don't need more good ideas. You need more bad ideas.**

Seth speaks from experience, having published dozens of books, including several bestsellers, and having presented TED talks with tens of millions of views. It's no coincidence that Seth posts daily to his blog (as do I, which helped create this book). A few pages later, Seth used director Sam Raimi to describe a similar pattern:

Raimi is one of the most successful directors of his generation (*Spider-Man, Darkman, Evil Dead*, etc.).

As a teenager, and later in film school, he insisted on screening his films to a paying audience. "Fifty cents, a dollar, it didn't matter, as long as they paid something."

He discovered early on that paying audiences cared more and demanded more.

Again and again, his work was booed and met with derision.

So he'd go back to the editing room and edit the film. He'd make the scary parts scarier, the funny parts funnier, and then he'd do it again.

Sooner or later, Sam Raimi was making movies.

"Sure," you might say. "Isaac, Seth, and Josh probably loved writing and Sam probably loved making movies. If I had a passion, I'd do it daily too. Then I could create bad ideas and turn them into good ones."

You likely don't yet have a life passion—something you jump out of bed for, creating boundless energy, supportive community, independence from resource constraints, security, freedom from others' judgment, confidence, and recognition for your efforts.

If a passion brought you money, power, and fame along the way, you probably wouldn't mind, but its greatest reward would likely come from serving others you care about.

Most people live passionless lives, giving up on developing it. Yet others jump from passion to greater passion, never giving up when a passion doesn't pan out. The passion-to-passion-never-giving-up group is as human as you. Method Initiative will make you one of them.

The path isn't as simple as starting with passion. Nor is the path to act without passion. Paradoxically, most of us sense no passions, too many, or both none and too many at once. Understanding why will prepare us for the exercises in Part Two.

Passions, Interests, and Passing Fancies

Life has many passing fancies, some meaningful interests, and few life passions. I think of them in a hierarchy like this:

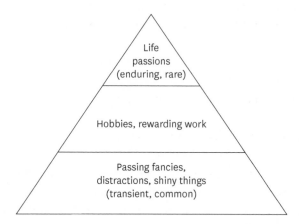

Passing fancies are things we enjoy in the moment but don't bring long-term emotional reward. Since everyone's values differ, your passing fancies will differ from mine. Our world is full of passing fancies like social media, fun classes, action movies, and some friendships. Our culture bombards us with more. From grade school through commencement, mainstream education spreads us thin with classes, extracurriculars, double majors, triple minors, sports, after-school jobs, and so on—too thin to go into depth with any of them. Most jobs continue the pattern.

Rarely do you act on your own interests enough to distinguish what you care about. Choosing a major or job hardly lets you explore your interests. Nor does starting a company in a Dog Show culture. Meanwhile, marketers have learned to attract our attention. If they find out you like yoga, they'll pitch you meditation, clothes, retreats, and the whole lifestyle. Same with cars, books, travel, or any other interest. Social media compounds the distractions.

The problem isn't that those things aren't valuable. It's that they *are*, but we have finite resources. People who content themselves with unexamined lives, passively enjoying what others present to them, rarely find enduring, deep reward.

Meaningful interests, meanwhile, include hobbies, rewarding work, and things that bring long-term emotional reward, but not things that you'd devote your life to. Mine include cooking, my windowsill garden, some challenging courses, and closer friendships. Meaningful interests are candidates for life passions, though not the only source.

Life passions inspire us, giving us boundless energy. The challenge with life passions isn't knowing what a passion is in principle, but identifying our own with enough confidence to choose them over competing interests and passing fancies. Once you commit to a life passion, you see passing fancies as leeches, sucking energy, time, and other resources from it. When you have nothing better, drinks after work with coworkers sounds fun, but when you're a parent, you won't let casual drinks keep you from your child's recital.

How do we find and create life passions? Culture confuses us with the romantic idea that passion comes when muses whisper in our ears, the stars align, or we're born with it. Like love at first sight, such things may happen, but rarely enough to count on it. Believing passion *just happens* motivates waiting. Meanwhile, as with love, those who develop themselves and put themselves out there tend to find what they're looking for. Chance favors the prepared mind and passion favors the active life.

So what activity breeds passion? Method Initiative may not be the only way to create passion, but it works. As with love, I know of no way without ups, downs, and some heartbreak, but in the end you look back at the challenges and realize you needed them to learn what to reject as much as what to commit to.

Some people believe you need to start with a passion, which will motivate you to act:

Passion ——————— Leads to ———————➤ **Action**

Some hope a passion finds them by luck. Since passions rarely appear out of the blue, this view renders them helpless to act. They wait and hope, often their entire lives. Again, love at first sight may happen sometimes, but I wouldn't base my life on it.

Others believe you have to start by acting, which will lead you to discover passions. To the extent it presumes that taking an idea to business success will lead to you loving what you do, Lean works this way. It looks like this:

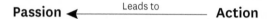

Passion ◄——————— Leads to ——————— **Action**

Some get lucky acting on this model. I followed this model with my first company. I loved developing an idea I conceived of and building a company, but couldn't develop a passion for outdoor advertising. Many people burn out after acting without finding passion, erroneously concluding they just aren't born entrepreneurs or initiators. They're more like someone who gets sore or injured their first time weightlifting. The problem wasn't lifting weights, but improper form, or lifting too much too soon.

Relying too much on passion or action puts too much burden on those factors. What works is what I call the Initiative-Action-Passion cycle:

Starting with a little initiative, perhaps directed by an awareness of a potential passion, may motivate some action—enough to see if it leads to more passion, but not enough to cause burnout. If you feel the passion increase, you'll feel motivated to take initiative to act more. I don't suggest vaguely to "find your passion" or "do your best." Method Initiative gives you specific steps that work. Passion directs your initiative. Initiative drives action. Action increases passion.

The more times you initiate and act, the more passion you'll build, which will motivate more initiative, continuing the cycle. Starting small means you don't have to wait for an outside muse, nor act in arbitrary directions or by following others' interests. Going around the cycle does more than bring you back to the start. Like a spiral staircase, each time around brings you to another level. Method Initiative elevates you from passing fancies to life passions.

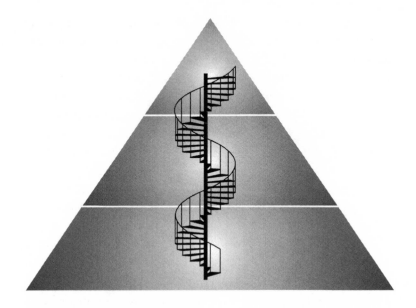

In fact, the entrance of the Louvre in Paris has such a spiral staircase in a pyramid elevating people from one level to the next:

The more times you implement Method Initiative, the more you leave passing fancies behind and live a life of passion. How many times you will to go through the ten exercises in Part Two depends on your situation. Growing up in New Orleans, surrounded by jazz, Louis Armstrong found his life passion by his teens. J.K. Rowling struggled through many endeavors before finding writing, and even then had to struggle before publishing *Harry Potter*. Alexander Calder showed interest in art as a youth, but had to work through interests in engineering and other fields to come back to it. After finding art, he had to go through a few cycles to discover abstract, kinetic art. Method Initiative enables you to follow paths like theirs.

One question remains: if you begin with initiative before you know your passion, how do you choose direction for your first iteration of the cycle? If you feel you don't have any passions, you lack direction. If you feel you have too many passions, you fear moving in a direction you'll regret if you later find you *really* loved a different option. Most cases of people feeling they lack passion arise from this fear obscuring multiple candidate interests. I mentioned how passing fancies leech our energies. All candidates for passions, even rewarding hobbies, distract or paralyze us if we lack the skills to liberate ourselves from their grips.

To answer how to choose direction, I bring up the last, beautiful, liberating main ingredient to Method Initiative: *exhausting interests*.

Exhausting Interests

In your teens, did you love bands that you later cringed at? I did. I played the same songs over and over until the needle in my plastic record player dulled the groove. By high school, I had exhausted my interest in those bands. They led my tastes to mature to the point where I would have felt embarrassed if my friends knew I had listened to them.

Today I understand that I was too young to have developed taste in music and my high school friends had probably cringed at their earlier tastes too. I had to listen to what I liked at first to mature.

A similar pattern happened in college. I started majoring in architecture. My dad loved the field and nudged me toward it. I saw an elegance in it. I put a lot into it until I exhausted my interest in architecture. In fact, I felt architecture overly favored design over physics—part of what motivated me toward majoring in physics, which I loved.

I later exhausted my love for physics, at least as practiced today, which fostered my passion for active, experiential, project-based learning. As with music, trying and exhausting each interest not only *led* to a greater interest, it was actually the *only way* to reach that greater interest. Looking at the passions of your role models, heroes, or friends won't tell you yours. Dabbling in an interest won't do it. A minimum level of commitment is necessary. Exhausting interests is an essential step in discovering passions. It's liberating to replace internal conflict, doubt, and insecurity with purpose, confidence, and security. It's part of maturing from an ineffective dilettante to an effective initiator.

Since our passing fancies and meaningful interests outnumber our potential passions by a wide margin, almost nobody will hit a life passion their first time taking initiative. But everyone who takes initiative, even if they have to exhaust several candidate interests, wishes they had acted earlier, knowing they'd have to spend all those resources on those candidate interests.

However torn you may feel between two interests, fearing acting on A because you might later find you love B more, acting on either will lead you to a life passion faster than analyzing and planning (sadly, what mainstream education teaches). If you choose A and end up loving it, congratulations. If you actually love B more, acting on A will cause it to lose its luster faster and more surely than any other technique. Acting on A will give you the skills and sensitivity to sense your greater passion for B. You will love B more for exhausting A. You will feel gratitude for A and the work you put into it for bringing you to B.

Climbing the spiral staircase with any interest will take you out of the realm of passing fancies and distractions. Switching projects is like switching to another staircase that goes higher. Restarting the exercises from the start doesn't mean you descend when the new project connects to greater passion. Climbing a turn or two makes you less likely to descend again even if that staircase tops out. It also enables you to see staircases you couldn't see from the bottom. Passion leads you to take more initiative, which leads you to act more, which increases your passion.

Many don't act out of fear of regretting a wrong choice, unwittingly risking never realizing a passion. Those who did act on an interest they later exhausted look back with gratitude at their "wrong" choice for having led to their passion. They realize that only by acting could they have found the limitations of the "wrong" choice's appeal.

The upshot for you is that your first choice for direction your first time trying Method Initiative has low stakes. Any choice will start a process that will lead to a life passion faster and more efficiently. The skills, experiences, and beliefs you develop in each iteration, including the first, will increase your sensitivity to latent interests. You will reject exhausted interests with greater surety. In fact, with each interest you reject, you will reject entire categories of interest. For example, say you find and act on an interest because it seems popular, but then realize popularity alone isn't enough for you. You'll likely no longer find any merely popular interest attractive. You'll look at people pursuing merely popular interests as still searching.

The exercises incorporate this pattern through the option to switch at any time. You will likely not have spent any money. You'll know that the idea of a lifetime comes once a month. Each time acting on an interest will develop you more, with some ups and downs, but generally toward greater passion and more confidently exhausting interests. You'll sense success sooner.

You can see the pattern of cautious attempts followed by passion in the students and clients profiled in this book. Grace and RJ were tentative before their ideas formed, then they committed confidently and enthusiastically. Esther changed direction after a year of law school. Andreas exhausted travel and seeking in a few months, then found more entrepreneurial passion in unexpected places than he could have without acting on candidate passions that didn't pan out themselves.

JOSHUA, PART 3

I love my podcast. I put my heart and soul into it. Beyond what you hear, tons of work goes into finding and booking guests, editing, creating events, and everything else behind the scenes. It's part of what I intend to make into a movement. It follows years of living the environmental values I believe most of us share—stewardship; clean air, water, and land; delicious food; personal growth; and so on. My goal is to share the joy, meaning, value, purpose, and passion I find in my environmental behavior that I see missing amid the coercion, compliance, facts, doom, and gloom in mainstream environmental communications.

It wasn't always as joyful. It began with initiative, building on two passions, lots of advice, and iteration.

One passion, science, to me is rooted in discovering and sharing the beauty of nature. As long as I can remember I've worked to preserve that beauty on a personal level—turning off lights when I leave a room, preferring public transit to cars, and so on.

The other passion, leadership, emerged from taking classes in business school after being squeezed out of my first company.

Science is nerdy. Leadership sounds lofty, but in practice, working with aspiring leaders means working in the trenches of people's challenges and flaws.

I considered my passions for nature and leadership unrelated until recently. My starting the *Leadership and the Environment* podcast in 2017 illustrates the process of developing a greater passion.

A few years ago, I began increasing my environmental stewardship, for example, challenging myself to avoid food packaging. I was acting on an interest. I expected the change to feel like deprivation, but to my surprise, I found the opposite. Within months, cooking from scratch became more delicious, cost less, saved time, and connected me with my family, community, and local farms. Several other changes led to similar results. Where I expected sacrifice, I found joy, saving time and money, community connection, and more results I liked.

My activity led me to see leadership missing from environmentalism. I don't consider people telling others what to do, or spreading facts, information, and doom and gloom leadership. I saw a need for a Mandela of the environment. While it still feels presumptuous to say it, if a Mandela of the environment is what I felt was most missing, and if no one else was doing it, I decided I would try. That gumption forced me to wrestle with the risk of looking foolish or publicly failing. I felt torn, not impassioned.

I acted with what I could. First I spoke to friends about my interest, soliciting suggestions. I gave a series of talks at NYU and Columbia that I expected to inspire. Instead, they revealed my ignorance of the emotional minefield speakers face on the subject: people push back at a lot of environmental talk. The feedback from attendees discouraged me nearly to give up.

I kept working at the talks, though, listening to attendees' advice and experiences. Then a conversation with a former student inspired me back. Without my prompting, he decided to try my habit of picking up at least one piece of trash per day, having heard how I'd come to enjoy the habit. He committed to picking up ten pieces of trash per day for a month. At the end of the month, he told me he enjoyed the habit enough to find more to act on his environmental values. He cut his meat intake by half while meeting his dietary goals as a weightlifter. He acted out of joy and expectation of success, not coercion, facts, guilt, blame, doom, or gloom.

People talk about raising awareness to motivate behavior, but with environmental issues front page news for years, everyone is aware. I found that behavior led to awareness more than the other way around and that people tended to claim needing to raise awareness to delay acting. I decided to replicate what worked with him more publicly by starting a podcast with a format based on what worked. It still took some iterations to reach the current format: featuring influential people sharing their joy and reward from acting on their environmental values. I don't give them tasks. I ask them to share their personal environmental values, which I then invite them to act on share their experience. Since they create the task based on their values, they do it for themselves, not for me or out of coercion. I soon found support beyond any I expected when world-class influencers like Daniel H. Pink, Jonathan Haidt, and Seth Godin participated enthusiastically.

I felt inspired!

The next iteration came from talking to a guest, Sandy Reisky, who pointed me to research[2] showing that a top predictor of people installing solar on their homes, more than how much money they'd save or their politics, was how many neighbors had it. I concluded that community influenced social and cultural change more than facts, science, guilt, blame, doom, or gloom and decided to refine my strategy to bring guests in everyone's communities—renowned leaders. I'm not trying to use celebrity. I want to help people move from "If I act but no one else does then my actions won't mean anything" to "People in my community—people in *everyone's* community—are acting. Time for me to as well."

I couldn't have predicted finding a passion that clicked with so many things I cared about. Only acting on what I knew at the time could reveal it.

Do you see the cycle of finding ever greater passions and acting on them, each time developing more skills and sensitivity to deeper interests? I believe I will significantly change an area of unmet global demand. Time may reveal that I was mistaken and I don't influence much, but in the meantime, I work with influential people like Nobel laureates, #1 bestselling authors, Pulitzer Prize winners, a Presidential Medal of Freedom honoree, a Super Bowl champion, Olympic athletes including a gold medalist, Victoria's Secret models, sustainability teams at Fortune 100 companies, CEOs of publicly traded companies, and Hollywood directors, with more to come. My guests share joy based on experience, not guilt, blame, doom, gloom, or facts that don't motivate. I give them a platform to create environmental legacies. Since they have larger followings than I do, I'm helping them become Mandelas of the environment. I also face incredible frustration, along with people's inaction and misunderstanding, which I learn from.

I spent probably under $100 to start the podcast. I've since spent a few thousand dollars on back-end equipment and services, but it's created more speaking and coaching revenue, not to mention joy, growth, and connections.

I may seek investment to expand. If so, it will be to serve my listeners and guests and will come from sources who want to help that mission. Who knows, I may win my equivalent of Best in Show, but that would be a side effect. If I do, it will mean I've influenced hundreds of millions of people to find joy, meaning, value, importance, purpose, and passion, where they now feel lethargy, complacency, and indifference—in stewardship, cleanliness, purity, responsibility, and maturity. It will have come from loving my Jake.

TWO

METHOD INITIATIVE: THE EXERCISES

OVERVIEW

Strategy

Method Initiative is a comprehensive progression of exercises that leads you to master the social and emotional skills, experiences, and beliefs of taking initiative to help others so they reward you for it. In the process you will create a supportive community, including valuable people in your field. You can repeat the exercises as often as you like, each time creating more passion, focus, self-awareness, results, community, and freedom from distraction.

You will likely exhaust the interest you start with the first time you practice the exercises. I recommend that you prepare for this potentiality by making your first-time goal to develop skills, experiences, and beliefs, which will help you choose a candidate interest you like more the next time. You will sense your skills developing, which you will likely find rewarding.

If your first time leads to a passion, great! Enjoy jumping out of bed. I'd love to hear from you about it. Otherwise, in the next cycles, interests will last longer (or you'll exhaust them faster) and create more meaning, value, and purpose. You'll need less willpower as your experience tells you to expect success sooner. You will choose interests to act on with greater confidence from a smaller pool that you value more.

Experience will make subsequent cycles easier, faster, more fun, and more rewarding. Your results will be more meaningful, valuable, purposeful, and passionate. You'll value the people you serve and work with. They'll value you in return.

Even your first time finishing all ten exercises will lead to an enduring project. It may become a Best in Show that brings you fame and fortune, or just your Jake that you love and that rewards you back. Either way, you will enjoy the process and be able to repeat it for the rest of your life.

Jonathan, for example, exhausted corporate law and is disrupting a field, working with titans of industry, and helping people that society abandoned. Chris exhausted entrepreneurial practices he now finds impersonal in favor of more human and meaningful relationships. Andreas exhausted traditional entrepreneurship despite his success in it, and abandoned the Dog Show in favor of activities he would pay to do, uninhibited by what others may think.

People who find a passion and exhaust their almost-passions wish they had acted earlier. To view passing fancies as leeches clarifies your purpose and liberates you from them—one of the greatest liberations you can experience in life. You learn how much more you can do. It focuses you. You see the grip that ephemeral urges and cravings have on most people, but no longer on you. You free yourself from monkey mind.

Instead of agonizing over what to do, analyzing trivialities, and complaining, you confidently and deliberately make time for what you want. It's a different world.

Tactics

To learn to play the piano, you might consider a class in music appreciation. You'd learn about Bach, Beethoven, and Ellington, some music theory and such, but if you want to play, you have to put your fingers on the keys. Appreciation may not hurt, but it won't help you play.

Most books, courses, TED talks, and other resources on initiative or entrepreneurship are on *appreciation*. It's nice to learn principles, but as I wrote in chapter 5, if you want to develop skills in ASEEP fields, you have to practice the basics, and initiative and entrepreneurship are ASEEP fields.

Have you noticed the amount of business literature by and about Navy SEALs? Navy SEALs don't train by reading those books and articles. That's SEAL *appreciation*. If SEAL appreciation developed SEALs, they'd train that way. They don't because it doesn't. They train by practicing.

Playing scales isn't banging keys randomly. Masters in any Method Field developed and tested exercises over generations. Tennis players start with ground strokes; the military begins with basic training. Method Initiative puts your hands on the keys of initiating and entrepreneurship.

The main tactic is to do the exercises as described. You might worry about your authentic voice and style emerging if you follow the same instructions as everyone—but remember the quote from Martha Graham in chapter 5: "Freedom may only be achieved through discipline." Sticking to your craft is your best route to freedom of expression. You won't learn piano practicing scales as do re fa mi la so ti. Playing the same scales as everyone is the fastest way to mastery, including improvisation, and so is practicing Method Initiative by the book the first few times. You'll be surprised by how fast your voice and style emerge.

I recommend starting sooner, not later. You can do most of the first exercise before you go to sleep tonight. Many people give reasons to wait—inexperience, lack of passion, fears, anxieties, myths, and the hurdles I listed in earlier chapters. Success comes from seeing them as reasons to act, not to wait. Inexperience is a reason to *start* Method Initiative, not to wait. Lack of passion is a reason to *start* Method Initiative, not to wait. Same with fear, anxiety, lack of resources, and so on. Method Initiative solves those problems with small steps.

You can do the exercises alone or with others, either working on a joint project or creating independent projects in different fields and learning from each other as you go through the same process. You're learning similar social and emotional skills—in the way piano students learning jazz, classical, or pop all start with the same scales.

Basics doesn't mean only for beginners. LeBron James hasn't outgrown practicing jump shots, nor Serena Williams ground strokes. On the contrary, they practice them before their most important performances. These exercises are like cardiovascular exercises that help in all sports. Masters of all fields know that the more difficult a situation, the more valuable technique is and the more they rely on the basics. Want to do fancy spin moves in salsa? Practice your footwork. Want to inspire employees and investors? Practice Method Initiative.

However simple a given exercise looks, each builds to the next, so I recommend not skipping steps or doing them perfunctorily. I've removed everything inessential. If it looks easy, there's no harm in doing it fast, but do each conscientiously and diligently.

In Rafael's words, "Josh's approach and philosophy is very experiential. For example, you don't become an entrepreneur by reading about entrepreneurship; you don't become a better runner by watching movies about running. You become a better salesperson by picking up the phone or going out and talking to people; you become a better runner by putting on your running shoes and putting one foot in front of the other. The approach and methodology are not theoretical."

Process

Watch grade school students performing—say, sprinting—and you'll see lots of extraneous motion. Their expressions show they are trying hard but their flailing bodies show they are wasting energy. Desire isn't enough.

Watch Olympic athletes sprint. Their faces are focused. Their form shows no extraneous motion. Every part of their bodies is moving toward the finish line or moving back to propel the rest forward.

Mastery comes from disciplined practice and rehearsal. Whether athletic, or any other performance, masters worked on every element of their craft through practicing exercises. While Method exercises in many fields may look just physical, they develop skills, experiences, and beliefs in their bodies, minds, and hearts. They develop self-awareness, authentic self-expression, confidence, and more.

Some beginners look at masters and say, "I could never perform like that." They use their undisciplined form as an excuse not to try. Like it or not, the only way to mastery is to start by flailing like a grade school kid. Lack of technique is a reason to practice and rehearse *more*, not less.

This rest of this book presents ten exercises to train you to whatever level of mastery you want in taking initiative. While there's no harm in reading them all through before starting, the way to do them is to 1) do one exercise, 2) reflect on it and write your reflections, and 3) do the next exercise. Repeat until the last exercise, or, if you exhaust an interest, restart and repeat the cycle with a new one.

Structure

Each exercise starts with a general description followed by an Action section specifying what to do, using a checklist and describing the deliverables.

The Post-exercise Reflection section suggests ideas and questions to consider. You learn by doing. Reflection surfaces more and leads you to retain what you learned and generalize it, and prepares you to apply it next time.

I recommend posting your reflections to a public blog because public accountability makes you reflect more thoughtfully. You can keep it anonymous if you like. I recommend at least finding a supportive friend or family member to read your reflections. The online version of the course at spodekacademy.com offers a forum where only participants can see each other's reflections. It's a supportive community of like-minded learners and practitioners where everyone flails and learns from each other.

Again, the short-term result of doing the exercises will be a project you love, helping people you care about solve a problem, and creating a community of valuable people who support you. The long-term results will be the ability to start projects in general, greater self-awareness, and the ability to act on it.

These exercises aren't secrets. They teach you solid, basic, effective social and emotional skills of creating and operating effective projects. They aren't magic. They work.

Time and Money

Your pace and schedule are up to you. When I teach the course in corporations and universities, I assign an exercise per week. Some participants doing them solo finish in about a month. Others have taken over six months, choosing to focus on some areas more, or because their project demanded it. I've taught the course block-week style, meaning 9 a.m. to 5 p.m. for a week, with homework each evening. The experience is intense and creates a tight cohort, and everyone gains from the experience.

As for budget, many do the exercises without spending a dime. You need no special equipment.

The Mountaintop

The last exercise—speaking to valuable people in your field as a peer—is the big one. If you've done all the steps leading to it, they will treat you as a peer and help you, feeling a vested interest in your success. Many students are surprised at how fast they earn support from people at the frontiers of their fields. They have to remind themselves that these valuable people don't know that their ideas or expertise may not have existed a month before. But people who see you as a problem solver who initiates effectively want you around. You improve their lives and communities.

If, after finishing the exercises, you find that your project can use entrepreneurial management skills, you may find learning Lean or Design Thinking helps, though you may also feel that you've passed that stage and can hire people to manage for you, as you might hire an accountant or a lawyer.

Shouldn't I Form a Team?

Many students ask if they should form a team for the exercises. After all, isn't entrepreneurship a team effort? Isn't the point of taking initiative to help others?

If you want to play an instrument in a band or orchestra, to play a team sport, or to perform in top organizations, you first have to master your instrument or your game.

Mastering your instrument will attract other top performers to play with you and hire you. If you don't master yours, you won't play well with others. If you do, you'll attract teammates who share your passion and level of action. Method Initiative is the initiative equivalent of mastering your instrument.

If you have teammates or acquire them through the exercises, feel free to include them, but not obliged.

A Word on Reflection

Many people who finished the exercises describe their reflections as the most important part of the course. Research shows that reflecting on experience helps you retain what you've learned and apply it beyond that one experience.

I recommend reflecting on the seven principles after each exercise. They will take on new meaning and importance with practice. It's tempting to skip reflecting, but I'll quote Harvard Business School research[1] that looked at performance in 30-day corporate training programs comparable to Method Initiative. One group did the program as usual. The other spent 15 minutes each day reflecting and writing that day's main lessons. They found that a mere 15 minutes per day led to a 23-percent boost in performance. In their words, "reflecting after completing tasks is no idle pursuit: it can powerfully enhance the learning process. Learning, we find, can be augmented if one deliberately focuses on thinking about what one has been doing." Reflecting on what you do teaches you to do better next time.

The performance boost comes from feeling more competent and confident about your capability in performing that task. The study found that you don't need fancy tools—just to write.

Low-Level Details

"Okay, Josh," you ask. "But what do I actually *do*?"

You'll see that the first exercise is to write a personal essay. After reading that exercise, I recommend one of three first steps.

Option one is to get out a piece of paper and pen or to open your computer and start the essay. The advantage of this option is that you can start immediately and it costs nothing. Its downside is that it lacks feedback and the motivation of public accountability.

Option two is to create an account with any blog service and start the essay there. This option is also free. You can make the blog anonymous or not, as you prefer. You can choose whom you tell about it.

Option three is to sign up for the online course at spodek academy.com and start writing the essay on the forum there. This option is not free, but the code INITIATIVEBOOK will get you a 25-percent discount. More importantly, the forum is populated by people going through the same process as you, so you can ask, share, and learn from each other's experiences. It also contains videos of me describing the exercises, and emails you reminders to stay on track.

Once you get out that paper or create that account, you'll find continuing easier.

Examples

The online and in-person versions of the course give you access to the reflections of everyone who did them there before, and you can interact with those peers. You can read theirs and they can read yours, which may sound scary, but participants love and value it. Knowing others will read your reflections forces you to reflect more deeply and write more clearly, which leads to more learning and effective action.

Even one person's reflections could fill a book, but I'll share a few highlights from a couple of participants to illustrate their experiences and motivate you. Keep in mind, you're reading a small fraction of their total reflections.

CHRIS

Chris teaches at the University of Southern California and uses my first book, *Leadership Step by Step*, in his courses. At least that's what I learned about him when a colleague at usc introduced us. Chris told me he was interested in my course and signed up to take it online.

I first looked up Chris's full background while writing this book. Had I known his experience, I might have felt nervous about so experienced an entrepreneur taking my course.

If anyone can compare Method Initiative with Design Thinking and Lean, Chris can.

From his LinkedIn profile:

I am a startup founder, software executive, consultant and former **USC** professor. I have led 50+ products and business initiatives for companies that include Disney, Microsoft, Sony, Acclaim, Activision, BBC, Discovery, Children's Television Workshop, and many others. Game examples include the world's first massively multiplayer casual game, NetWits (Microsoft), the original Multiplayer Jeopardy! Online (Sony), the original Multiplayer Wheel of Fortune Online (Sony), and webRIOT (MTV).

I co-directed the Electronic Arts Game Innovation Lab at USC and was a founding faculty member in the USC Games program. USC Games is consistently the #1 ranked college game program by Princeton Review. While at USC I also co-authored the book *Game Design Workshop*, which has become the leading college game text. Prior to USC I was a founding member of the digital agency R/GA Interactive in NY. We grew R/GA Interactive from 4–100+ people and $0 → $50mm in revenue during my time there.

I speak regularly about startups and game innovation in the press and at events around the world. Publications include CNN, NPR, Forbes, NY Times, Wired, Chicago Tribune, Washington Post, LA Times, others. Venues include Game Developer's Conference, MIT, Harvard, SIGGRAPH, University of Tokyo, Games for Change, DARPA, Columbia University, Sorbonne, City U of Hong Kong, many others.

Specialties: Lean methodology, Agile development, digital marketing, SEO/SEM, game innovation, playable system design, strategic design, team building.

Holy cow! Chris's Wikipedia page adds more, including serving on the Board of Directors of the Academy of Television Arts & Sciences (the Emmys) and being awarded *Time Magazine*'s Best of the Web.

Chris knows entrepreneurship and initiative.

Chris did the Method Initiative exercises online. He began with a general idea of a project. He had the experience to use Lean or another methodology but chose to try Method Initiative. He worked at his own pace, sometimes spending weeks on one exercise, or a few days on others.

As of this writing, Chris is working on the last exercise. He has created meaningful connections with valuable people, with upcoming presentations for meaningful deals to bring his project to profitability.

He says, "This course has transformed my mindset about the entrepreneurial process . . . In my previous ventures I used a very inward-facing creation process and was constantly frustrated and personally overworked. I am embracing the outward-facing creation process from the course and have built great momentum and a group of people are engaging and moving the project forward."

During the course, Chris wrote extensive, thoughtful reflections to each exercise, which he shared on the online forum. Here are some highlights of his reflections, which make up maybe 10 percent of all he wrote:

Taking this course will hopefully be valuable because it will...
- Take me out of my comfort zone in areas where I need to improve and practice
- Take me down a practical path to creating my venture
- Keep my thoughts about execution at speed at front of mind

What is your field of interest?
Location-based augmented reality

How did you feel during the conversations? How did the other people seem to feel?
Requesting feedback creates a completely different dynamic from pitching. I was more relaxed and humble and the interviewees were also more relaxed and friendly. I have historically had a hang-up about asking people for help, and that hang-up has affected me negatively throughout my career. So this exercise provides excellent practice for me to understand how to ask for help. I have already switched my default approach to one of asking for feedback when I am trying to accomplish anything with people. And I am marveling at how effective it is in any situation (boss, co-workers, spouse, children).

Did you get advice beyond your expectations? Did you learn from the conversations?
Definitely. One of the things I learned was the value of seeking feedback from a diversity of types of people.

Do you feel your understanding of the problem and the quality of the solution improved?
Definitely. Surprisingly, even though the feedback was not from investor types the changes to the problem/solution led to better positioning for investor types.

Do you think the people you talked to are interested in learning how the project evolves?
Definitely.

How would you characterize the conversations—boring, fun, exciting, et cetera?
The words that come to mind are:
1. Authentic
2. Warm
3. Helpful
4. Positive
5. Bonding

Extremely valuable exercise!

His reflections on the next exercise, "5 People Who Feel the Problem," showed what looked to me like personal growth, increasing engagement, and enthusiasm beyond what looks like a simple exercise. Among his reflections, he answered the following questions:

How did you feel about the exercise before starting? Were you anxious, excited, confused, et cetera?
I felt positive all the way through. Not anxious.

How did your feelings change as you did the exercise?
Doing this makes me want to figure out how to segment the audience and try to get more data. I wrote a leasing agreement customized for my product and need to vet it with mall

leasing managers. Also I need to get data from retailers and include that in my deck. I also need to talk to high school and college kids and childless urban 25- to 35-year-olds about what they would and wouldn't do.

How did you feel during the conversations? How did the other people seem to feel?
All positives. It is imperative that you get candid feedback from potential users as opposed to cheerleading feedback. I have a UX background so get how to do it but usually don't do it on entrepreneurial ideas.

Do you feel differently about your project?
More engaged.

Has your motivation changed?
More motivated.

Do you feel your understanding of the problem and the quality of the solution have improved?
Definitely. Need to get polished mockups—marketing copy, kiosk design, storyboard of experience—in front of customers. This in order to get a more specific customer profile.

Do you think the people you talked to are interested in learning how the project evolves?
Yes.

How would you characterize the conversations—boring, fun, exciting, et cetera?
Warm. Interesting. Frank.
    Great exercise.

In response to exercise 8, "Details, Sustainability, and Financials," Chris said the following:

The exercise forced me to do a lot of research into the costs of team personnel, vendors, and venues (malls). I had to speak to about two dozen people to do this and have about 40 pages of notes referencing the numbers in the spreadsheet.

Each iteration had problem areas that were a result of dubious assumptions on my part. These dubious assumptions were almost always a case of being overly optimistic about the amount of staff needed or the amount of time needed to accomplish different tasks. I was pretty good at estimating costs for salaries and vendors but needed to build in more people and more time. The conversations I had as part of the exercises exposed me to people who questioned my assumptions about monthly ticket sales per venue. They led me to different people who could educate me about the different classifications of malls used in the retail industry and the real foot traffic data for each classification. Now key assumptions in my financials are backed up by sources. This layer of credibility entirely changes the conversation about my venture. While the hockey stick [that is, a business whose profits are flat for a long time, like a hockey stick shaft, then rise suddenly like the blade] is flatter in later iterations, the pro forma [financials] is now much more persuasive.

The exercises forced me to speak with lots of others. Those conversations led to recruiting a great team of programmers and business partners interested in taking the concept to investors.

Starting with a visual model makes making the financials easier, as Chris found when he had made his financials first:

In retrospect, doing this exercise ["Create a Visual Model"] before doing a pro forma would be a much more efficient sequence to get a complete picture of what the business needs. In the way it worked out this time my diagram is a reflection of my pro forma doc. In the future it will be more efficient to make the diagram first and then make the pro forma as a reflection of the diagram.

Many people say that business is about people and relationships. I agree, though in my experience, few live up to that principle. Chris's language—*authentic, warm, helpful, positive, bonding, interesting, frank*—illustrates how Method Initiative teaches practicing it.

He creates meaningful connections with valuable people, and he has upcoming presentations for meaningful deals to bring his project to profitability.

He also wrote: "I see Method Initiative as a first step, Design Thinking as a second, and Lean + Agile as a third."

And: "Since starting the course I have focused attention on the human communication aspects of being an entrepreneur as mentioned in the essay in exercise 1. I'm pleased to be making strides in this regard. For example, six great people are working on the project besides me. All six are stronger in their respective roles than the corresponding people who worked on my previous venture."

RITA

Rita is a model-turned-entrepreneur who has worked in fashion since her teens. Taking my course as a professional, she applied the Method Initiative exercises to a company she had already started.

She did them in just over a month. Along the way she grew in excitement, confidence, and passion, as you'll see in her reflections, which show one of the most telltale signs of passion: loving what from the outside looks like grunt work.

At the end of the exercises, she wrote, "Quite a bit has changed for me over the last five weeks. My project has developed and evolved into something that I'm interested in pursuing this year. I have never felt so excited about an idea and I feel more equipped from the knowledge I have gained through the advice of friends, family, and peers, as well as in class discussions with Josh and the exercises."

She continued: "Although starting this business will be a change of course . . . I'm excited to use my expertise as a personal stylist and working in women's wear for the last 12 years. I feel the need to start something that truly does solve a problem, and when I speak with women who are feeling the problem I want to start right away.

"The next steps are daunting," she continued, "as I have never designed a website and had one built with so many moving parts or approached investors before. However, I have gained more confidence that I can do it."

Here is an example of Rita's reflection on exercise 4:

I felt really excited to share my problem and solution with my friends and family. Many of them noted that my excitement was contagious and they got excited as well, since many of them could see themselves having the problem and wanting a solution.

And from exercise 5:

Each time I spoke with someone, my confidence did grow and many of the pieces of advice were very helpful to reshape the problem/solution. I gained a better understanding the more people I spoke with, especially from the more mature female demographic.

From exercise 6:

At the beginning of each exercise, I felt some anxiety to talk with people about my idea, especially people in my field, but after each week I felt so good and even more motivated to find out more. I have to remember where I started, and turn that anxiety into excitement.

From exercise 8:

This was such a fun exercise! It was so satisfying to have all the numbers mapped out like this. I feel I have a better handle on where to spend the money and where I can cut back. I found it amazing how lowering a monthly cost even by $25 a month really affected the accumulated profit. I'm now motivated to talk with programmers and get a better idea of the cost and how I could save on this expense without losing quality.

UNIT 1

YOU AND A PROBLEM YOU CARE ABOUT

EXERCISE 1
Personal Essay

W E BEGIN WITH a straightforward first exercise: a personal essay on yourself, and on initiative, entrepreneurship, responsibility, why you decided to take this course, and a field of interest to you. The personal essay has several goals:

1. To lead you to reflect on what brought you here.
2. To direct your focus to a field you're interested in.
3. For future reference, as you may develop more than you expect.
4. To introduce yourself to whoever reads your reflections, if you choose to share them.

I recommend 500 to 1,000 words, but write as much as you like. As for what to write about, something motivated you to pick up this book. I suggest starting with that. The more you clarify that motivation, the easier you will find the exercises, and writing clarifies thought. I also listed further starting points in the Action section that follows.

Within the essay, include at least one field of interest. You can change it later, but get something on the page. At this stage you can be as vague as "something with people" or as specific as "high-energy particle physics."

If this is your first time, remember that your choice is low-stakes. You'll likely exhaust it in favor of one you like more, looking back at this one with gratitude for leading you to the new one. The idea of a lifetime comes once a month.

Along with the main essay, create three lists of three people:

1. For the first list, name three people closer to your field of interest. Feel free to interpret this broadly. If you're thinking of making an app for music, for example, you could include musicians, app designers, friends with lots of music apps, and so on.
2. For the second list, name three people with high status or value in your field.
3. For the third list, name three relevant role models. These three can be people who are living or historical.

For all three lists, name people, not positions like the CEO of some company.

After you make these lists, I recommend writing down the value of taking an experiential, exercise-based course in acting with initiative. I suggest a few sentences beginning with "Taking a course like this is valuable because..."

This first exercise does not directly teach new initiative-taking skills. But, besides focusing you, it will combine with the second personal essay in exercise 9 to help show your development, which will help you augment it. If, despite my assurances on its helping past students, it reminds you so much of compliance-based school exercises that it keeps you from starting, you can skip writing a whole essay, but I still recommend at least answering a few of the questions below and naming the people.

Action

You can write about what you want, but here are some questions and topics to consider:

- What motivated you to learn initiative?
- What do you hope or expect to come from learning initiative?
- What do you think about taking responsibility, taking initiative, solving problems, and creating projects?

- What are your models for how taking initiative and entrepreneurship work?
- Who are your role models?
- What has worked for you so far in creating projects? What hasn't?
- Where do you want to take initiative? To business, your social life, family, yourself?
- What is your relevant history of taking initiative, if any? This can be your first memories, other relevant memories, and so on.
- What is the value in taking a course like this?

After writing your essay, I recommend sleeping on it, rereading it, and editing it before moving on.

Checklist

- ☐ Did you sleep on the essay and edit it?
- ☐ Did you include a field of interest?
- ☐ Did you describe the value of taking a course like this, maybe beginning with "taking a course like this is valuable because..."?
- ☐ Did you write three lists of three names each?

Post-exercise Reflection

Before continuing, reinforce what you learned by reflecting. Put distractions away and spend a few minutes thinking about what you learned.

You can reflect on what you like, but here are some questions you might consider:

- Was it easy to think of your relevant experiences, goals, and role models?
- Have you thought of someone to share your reflections with?
- What's the point of naming people, not positions?

The 7 Principles

I'll list the seven principles after each exercise, since students' reflections on them change, often deeply, with experience as they complete them. Internalizing these principles often gives a simple, direct way to remember and implement the overall skills, experiences, and beliefs of Method Initiative.

1. Personality matters less than skills you can learn.
2. The idea of a lifetime comes once a month.
3. Better than a great idea is an okay idea plus market feedback, flexibility, and iterations.
4. Start where you are with what you have.
5. Pitch and they'll judge. Ask advice and they'll help.
6. The problem leads to the solution.
7. Almost nothing inspires like helping others so much that they reward you for it.

If these haven't taken on deep meaning after your first personal essay, it's still early.

EXERCISE 2
5 Unsolved Problems

NIKITA

Nikita took my class as a freshman. Like most students, she didn't know she would start a project, let alone have an idea to start with. She planned to go into her family business of maritime law, but chose to use the class to explore other interests. Creating a project exposes you to new fields and connects you to valuable people in them, after all. With little risk, why not?

I assign "5 Unsolved Problems" over a week, suggesting that students explore what comes up naturally in their lives. Nikita probably gave blood or visited a doctor or dentist in that week because she came back with an unsolved problem of trypanophobia, the fear of needles and injections. Frankly, when I heard her description, I thought she had bitten off more than she could chew, anticipating regulations and other complications. Her results made me glad I held my tongue.

Nikita's problem and solution were more technical than my students usually pick. The problem she landed on was: "The phobia of needles can evolve into a lifetime debilitating fear. Not only is there mental trepidation involved with this experience, this also often produces physiological responses including but not limited to fainting, a drop in blood pressure, and vomiting."

Her rudimentary solution: "To create a device that can block sensations of pain so you don't (or barely) even feel the needle piercing the skin. Since that is often the most daunting part of the experience, the instrument could pulsate and numb the area through vibrations and cooling."

Does the project sound like too much to you too? It was enough to seed the rest of the exercises. She later described the experience that emerged: "Before Josh's class and its weekly practical exercises, I thought of my position as an 18-year-old student as a hindrance to being taken seriously in business. Why would a CEO want to listen to the ideas I had to pitch—a freshman?"

She did the exercises as assigned. About later exercises, she said, "We began by pitching our unmet need/solution to our classmates, followed by our friends and family, followed by ten valuable people who could aid our project. The real jump in this experiential process came when we contacted two dream contacts and experts within our space to get their advice on our solutions. I contacted a medical tech company whose lead medical engineer provided me with valuable tools to aid my product development. She has become a great mentor for me."

Nikita negotiated a partnership with the firm to develop a product based on principles she thought of to block the painful sensations on the skin. Medical engineers reported to her—a teenager. She is moving onward with her goals of finalizing her prototype and seeing her product in stores. In the meantime, *Forbes* profiled her.[1]

Nikita said on the results of the exercises, "I pitched my solution to a medical technology company and, while I cannot yet give away the details of the agreement, as the venture is in its infancy, I can say that Josh's class was the first to develop in me a sense of intrepid resolve, which can only come from moving outside the classroom, speaking with community leaders, and having the strong convictions and educated risk-taking to pitch my ideas to leading members of the field I pursued through my venture."

She summed up the experience: "More than anything, I've learned that being a student is an asset. People are willing to listen to someone with a passion—especially a young person—and a plan to implement that passion into a solution for an unmet need."

The lesson I hope Nikita leaves you with is that your initial problem and solution can sound rudimentary and impractical, yet still act as the seed necessary for the rest of the exercises to work. RJ and Grace learned that lesson. Nikita didn't need to win a contest to contact the medical device company, nor did Grace to reach the founder of Governors Ball. Preparing for contests would have slowed them down and distracted them from creating relationships and acting on them.

Mark Zuckerberg, Sergey Brin, Larry Page, and countless other successful initiators learned similar lessons in their lives. Method Initiative enables you to follow paths like theirs as opposed to the Dog Show.

Exercise 2 is to think in the context of the field you wrote about in your personal essay and come up with five problems in that field. For each problem, write a potential solution, no matter how rudimentary, tentative, or silly. *That solution's quality or viability is not the point of the exercise.* The point is to identify problems and the people feeling them.

What makes a problem: a **situation** that causes **at least one person** to experience **an unwanted emotion or feeling**. Make sure you describe at least those three elements.

The problems don't have to be big or earth-shattering, just clear enough to identify people who feel them and what they feel.

This stage's problems and rudimentary solutions, however silly, embarrassing, or otherwise unacceptable they seem to you now, are the seeds for the next exercises, which will refine them, teach you to refine ideas in the future, and make you a peer of history's successful initiators. Those people also began with rudimentary ideas.

Example problems at this stage include: "I get bored waiting in line for my coffee," "tipping is annoying," "people are hungry and living in the street," and "parents worry about foods having ingredients that their kids are allergic to."

That level of stating problems for this exercise is fine, as were Nikita's and RJ's. Start with a sentence or two stating the problem from the perspective of someone who feels it. Go into more depth if you write abstractions like "coffee wait times are too long" or "unemployment is an increasing problem in this nation," which don't specify a person or how they feel. Unemployment can be a problem for the unemployed, for politicians, for police, and so on. Some economists might consider unemployment part of a healthy economy and see no problem with it. Whom did you mean and how do they feel? How you state the problem steers how you solve it.

"People need food" doesn't state a problem. It's closer to stating a solution. It doesn't state an emotion or feeling that people don't like. "People are hungry" is clearer. Clearer still is "public school students are hungry at the end of the school day." Understanding problems will keep you from getting stuck on one solution, which leads to pitching and forcing square pegs into round holes. It also inhibits learning from others. Early solutions aren't supposed to solve problems, but instead seed the process.

"People need food" suggests giving people food. But maybe helping them get jobs or education on nutrition would help more. Focusing on problems more than solutions at this stage will lead you to find ways solve them more effectively.

Not all problems will lead to solutions you want to work on. You'll narrow your focus later. For now we're developing your skills and seeding later exercises, which means getting five problem-solution pairs before moving to the next exercise.

Students who don't get the exercise focus on the solution. Decades of compliance-based education and Dog Show Entrepreneurship trained us to think and act that way. Everyone shifts to focusing on the problem eventually, but the sooner you do, the faster you'll find a solution people will reward you for, the more effectively your solutions will help them, and the more people you will attract to help you.

Most importantly, the more you'll feel motivated. Eventually you'll feel inspired. Another reason to avoid focusing on a solution at this stage is that pitching solutions makes people feel you're trying to help yourself, not others, which motivates them to question you instead of help you.

What if I already have an idea I want to work on?
Many people start with an idea they want to work on. Rita, Marco, and Chris did, for example. This exercise helps them as much as anyone else. Still state the problem your idea solves from the perspective of the people who feel it. Still also state at least four more, which can be as close as you like to the one you want to work on.

What if I need to keep my idea confidential?
Some people can't disclose an idea they want to keep secret for legal or competitive reasons.

These exercises teach you skills and give experience beyond one idea. If confidentiality prevents you from working on your desired problem first, I recommend doing the exercises on a different problem, which will develop your skills, experiences, and beliefs. Then you can apply them to your private project when you finish.

The idea of a lifetime comes once a month.

Action

1. List five problems in a field of interest, identifying people it affects and the unwanted emotions it causes.
2. Write a rudimentary solution for each.

Deliverables

1. A **list of five problems,** clearly written in at most a few sentences each, **plus a rudimentary solution for each,** also in a sentence or two. I'll call a problem-solution pair a *project* from now on.

Slides or presentations, no matter how visually appealing, distract from developing the skills, experiences, and beliefs of the early exercises and make the next exercises harder.

As Grace said in her Harvard talk, "I never thought that I would be doing something like this and it has been an incredible journey that has been more simple than I could ever, ever imagine. I think it's really important to remember that. It can be a really, really simple idea, a really simple email like the one I sent, a really simple program that can make a really huge difference."

Checklist

☐ Did you identify and write the five problems clearly?
☐ Did you identify the people feeling the problems and their unwanted emotions?
☐ Did you write the problems in at most a few sentences?
☐ Beyond the deliverables, are you ready to write your reflections on the experience?

Post-exercise Reflection

Before continuing, reinforce what you learned by reflecting. Put distractions away and spend a few minutes thinking about what you learned.

You can reflect on what you like, but here are some questions you might consider:

• How hard was it to identify problems?
• Was it easy or hard to see them from the perspective of the people they affect?
• Did it get easier with practice?
• Do you think your problems and solutions have much chance to become viable projects?

The 7 Principles

Some of the principles may have started taking on meaning.

1. Personality matters less than skills you can learn.
2. The idea of a lifetime comes once a month.
3. Better than a great idea is an okay idea plus market feedback, flexibility, and iterations.
4. Start where you are with what you have.
5. Pitch and they'll judge. Ask advice and they'll help.
6. The problem leads to the solution.
7. Almost nothing inspires like helping others so much that they reward you for it.

Speaking of the seven principles, as Nikita later reflected, "The one I find most powerful, and relevant years later, is 'Better than a great idea is an okay idea with flexibility, market feedback, and iterations.' Not only has this shone a guiding light on my social entrepreneurial endeavors, but also on my life as a whole."

She continued, "After leaving Josh's class, you will start to live—to embody—the principles in your daily life, such as 1) Entrepreneurship and leadership are teachable skills, 2) Better than a great idea is an okay idea with market feedback and flexibility, and 3) The idea of a lifetime comes once a month. It is surprising how applicable these notions are even in a non-entrepreneurial setting."

An anonymous student review said, "Prior to this course, I had no idea how much behind-the-scenes work goes into creating something from scratch. I thought that all successful entrepreneurs came up with a brilliant idea that made them rich. However, I learned that there is so much more than a brilliant idea that goes into starting a business. I agree with the statement that thinking of an okay idea and taking input from outside people really helps better your product or service."

INTERLUDE
SWITCHING PROJECTS

IF YOU'RE READING this book for the first time, you probably don't have one shining project calling out for you to start it, deciding against all others. More likely you have none and aren't sure if any are worth starting, or have many and fear regretting starting the wrong one.

If so, you're not alone. In fact, you're par for the course. RJ didn't start with a project worth support from the Dalai Lama and TEDx. He started with vague direction at best, confused with options to continue working in politics in DC or to drop out of school. Grace started without an idea. Chris started with several ideas. Esther exhausted her travel app.

It's hard to drop an interest, but over and over, people who let go of a lesser project, even one they loved, to free themselves for one they love more say they wish they had let go earlier. You know who else didn't start with the projects they ultimately devoted themselves to? The founders of Twitter, YouTube, Instagram, and PayPal, among countless others. Each iterated many times before discovering what worked. So did the Buddha.

More important than creating *a project* you love is the ability to create *projects* you love. Starting down any path and switching teaches through experience beyond anything I or anyone else could tell you.

I have found the best measure of a project's value is not how great it sounds at inception, but the number of iterations it went through based on useful feedback. Every great project evolved through many iterations.

How do you learn to iterate a project many times without fearing you'll waste your time or regret your choices? Understanding that the idea of a lifetime comes once a month gives you the freedom to try a project out and iterate, knowing that if it doesn't work out, you'll soon be able to replace it.

You mainly have to learn through experience. The rest of the exercises will lead you to iterate your project many times. Most iterations are small. They keep the project basically the same, but slightly improved.

But sometimes you have to start a new project and drop an old one. Without the freedom of knowing you can—even if you don't—you will hold back from committing to your current project enough to see it through its early stages. I've found it the fastest, most effective, least regretful way to find what you love.

The Switching Rule

You can switch any time to a new project. The rule is that if you switch to a new project, you have to start it from the beginning— this will prevent holes in its foundation.

The Results of the Switching Rule

As I mentioned to Esther in our office hour, you will find three main results from restarting.

First, you may temporarily feel like you're moving backward or want to give up. You'll feel this way at times anyway. Doing the exercises is hard when you feel this way, but they will get you past the feeling, like physical therapy after an injury.

Second, you will finish the exercises faster and more easily each time. You will find that you have internalized skills and beliefs that make the exercises simple and natural. The first time you ask advice from people you don't know, you likely had to overcome inhibitions.

The next time, you'll act with more enthusiasm and skill. What took a week or two you may now do in an afternoon, accomplishing more.

Third, after a switch you will enjoy the exercises more. Caring more leads you to commit more, which leads you to care more and connect more meaningfully with more valuable people, driving the Initiative-Action-Passion cycle that turns interests into passions.

The new project will feel more meaningful. You will feel more motivation. You'll wish you had started it earlier. If you work more hours, you will feel as if you're working less, or not working but having fun.

It bears repeating that when you exhaust a project, you often exhaust a *class* of projects, relegating them to the passing fancy category, no longer distractions. For example, if you find you chose a project mainly for the money and then find money alone was not worth it, exhausting that project may lead you to exhaust *all* projects based mainly on money. You'll see people chasing money as out-of-control or lacking self-awareness. I'm not suggesting you won't still value money or what led you to your first project, only that it won't control you. No matter what class you exhaust, you'll see your life as more purposeful for the decreased distraction.

You can only tell which you'll exhaust through experience, so I don't recommend avoiding any one project.

You will feel more confident. You will feel less as if you're working on an interesting project and increasingly as if you're doing what you've always wanted to. The people you work with will become friends. People will remark on the change.

You Don't Have to Switch

All that said, if you love a project, you don't have to switch.

5 Close Contacts

Y OU CAN ONLY see a problem firsthand from your perspective. But, however well you can solve it, learning others' perspectives can reveal new ways to understand and solve it. Teams generally outperform individuals.

You might not have a team yet, but this exercise will start developing your skills, experiences, and beliefs to attract people by sharing with them what you're working on and leading them to help you.

This exercise has you act on your projects in a structured way designed to avoid anxiety, generate support, and develop your skills. Your close contacts may give useful advice, but generally won't. Their advice is a minor part of this exercise. The major part is you practicing presenting, deflecting judgment, listening, and other skills for soliciting useful advice and building relationships.

Later exercises, in which you ask advice from people in your field—especially valuable ones—are not the place to do things you haven't practiced many times before. When valuable people ask you questions, you'll want to have practiced answering them. This exercise prepares you with those skills so you can present confidently.

Practice will lead you to mastery. You'll develop skills including:
- Leading conversations by initiating them and keeping them focused
- Keeping people focused and the business exchange concise

- Deflecting judgment
- Motivating people to give advice
- Handling unhelpful advice respectfully
- Enjoying talking about your projects

You'll also find communication patterns that people love to do, and prompting them will lead people to want to help you. They include:

- Hearing about entrepreneurial projects
- Giving advice
- Helping people they've advised succeed
- Hearing that their advice was acted on

Students are often surprised to learn that telling people about entrepreneurial projects and asking them for advice is less like asking a favor and more like giving a gift. People love hearing ideas from problem solvers and giving them advice.

One anonymous student review said, "In class I have learned unparalleled skills for networking and reaching out, which I could not be happier to have. I will go on to use these communication skills for many years to come. I have been in contact with the founder of a major app development agency, jewelers, and other people who have created startups similar to mine. Being able to talk to these people and getting their advice has offered me great insights on the processes of creating jewelry, making apps, and running a startup."

Consider times when someone respectfully asked for your advice and you gave it. Did you hope they'd act on it? Did you feel something like, "Now they're more likely to succeed, and it's because of my help"? Did you feel motivated to help them act on your advice?

Most of us feel vested in the success of people we advise. We feel honored that they came to us and made us feel like experts. Once they follow our advice, we want to help them, so that their success becomes ours.

These patterns happen as much with high-value people as with your close contacts. Seeing them here will prime you to see them everywhere.

You will develop experience in:

- Expecting interest from the people you approach
- Saying "thank you," even for unhelpful advice
- Deflecting judgment
- Presenting ideas concisely
- Leading interactions about your ideas

Later exercises will build on this exercise's results.

Action

1. List five people close to you likely to support you and unlikely to judge you. Family, friends, and colleagues can all work.
2. Meet with each in turn. Tell each about the projects from your last exercise.
3. Ask each for a piece of advice on each.
4. Ask each to vote for the project they like the most.
5. After getting votes from each, choose which project you'll work on for the rest of the exercises.

Describe the ideas conversationally, without presentations or slides. I recommend a sentence or two for each.

Conversing by email doesn't count for this exercise. You can schedule by email, and video or phone can work if necessary, but ideally meet in person.

Leading and structuring the conversations

I recommend starting the conversation with something like:

Hey, I wonder if you have a second. I came up with a few entre-preneurship ideas. They're early, so I wonder if you can help give me some advice on them.

You may be surprised by how much people enjoy hearing entrepreneurial ideas. Many students and clients tell me they're worried about taking people's time before doing this exercise. No one has said so after it.

If they agree, continue by saying:

Great. I value your advice, so thank you. I have five ideas. I'd like to describe all five quickly and then get your advice on each.

After describing them, say something like:

Now that I've described them, I wonder if you could give me a piece of advice on each.

Tips

I want to prepare you for three common distractions—judgment instead of advice, long digressions, and unhelpful advice. They don't always happen at this stage, but they will eventually. Spotting them and handling them will lead to more productive and enjoyable interactions and relationships.

Judgment inhibits a helpful relationship—often one person feels on high, looking down, arms crossed, the other trying to please. We want to avoid trying to improve a project like playing Battleship: you propose an idea and a judge says, "not good enough" without offering guidance to improve.

People are so used to being asked to judge and judging that they'll do it even if you didn't ask for it. They'll say things like:

"The first idea is best."

"Great job. You can do this."

"Number three is too hard."

Or variations thereof, none of which are advice.

I offer two practices to help people advise you instead of judge you. These practices will help broadly in many future exercises, and in life.

First, start the conversation by clearly saying you're looking for advice. Avoid saying, "What do you think of the ideas?" or "Do you think they're good?" Such questions lead them to judge you. They slip out by habit.

Many will still respond with judgment. If so, I recommend deflecting the judgment and leading them back to advising. Try saying:

> I appreciate that you think it's great [or bad or however they judged], but I'm looking for advice I can act on. I wonder if you could suggest a way to improve it.

Politely persist once or twice until they give advice. If they can't think of any, thank them for their time and help, put a different person on your list, and continue the exercise with the new person.

Likewise, you may inadvertently judge their advice too, which discourages their help, even judging it positively. (Think of a time someone asked you for help and then judged you. Did you feel something like, "You ask me for help and then judge me? Who do you think you are?")

If you find yourself feeling compelled to judge their advice, I recommend instead saying "thank you." Even if you think their advice is good, I recommend not saying so, as judging positively is still judging. However positive you intend your message, you risk prompting them to feel something like, "Hmm... you judged me positively this time, but next time it might be negative," or "You asked me for help and then judge me?"

The second distraction is **long digressions.** You'll often feel conflicting tugs—one to keep this conversation short to respect their time, the other to talk at length if they like what you're doing.

I recommend keeping the business part of the conversation to the first five or ten minutes. If they want to keep talking, keep that fun part separate, after the business part. If they feel strongly about something you present, they'll often want to talk about it. Say they like your third idea and start asking for details or sharing their thoughts but not advice. I recommend saying something like:

> I want to follow up on what you're saying. Since I have two more ideas to cover, I propose we finish those two and pick up where we left off on this one.

Spoken respectfully, maybe while writing what they said to show more attention, people generally appreciate you leading the conversation to respect their time and words.

Enjoy the conversations that this exercise prompts—so long as you finish the business part first. They'll feel their time was respected. Finishing the business part allows you to enjoy the fun part.

The third distraction is **unhelpful advice.**

I recommend responding to it by simply saying "thank you," silently recognizing that they did their best to help. You don't have to act on advice just because someone gives it to you.

Deliverables

The output from the "5 Unsolved Problems" exercise—the five projects—is the input to this one.

The deliverables for this exercise are:

1. A list of the **advice you got** that is relevant to the project.
2. An **improved version** of the projects based on that advice.
3. Your **reflections** on the experience.
4. **Votes from each person** on which idea they liked most.
5. Your choice of **which project you'll work on.**

Checklist

☐ Did you talk to five people?
☐ Did you get five pieces of advice and a vote from each of them?
☐ Did you choose one project to work on?
☐ Beyond the deliverables, are you ready to write your reflections on the experience?

Post-exercise Reflection

Before continuing, reinforce what you learned by reflecting. Put distractions away and spend a few minutes thinking about what you learned.

You can reflect on what you like, but here are some questions you might consider:

- How did you feel about the exercise before starting? Were you anxious, excited, confused?
- How did your feelings change as you did the exercise?
- How did you feel during the conversations? How did the other people seem to feel?
- Did you get advice beyond your expectations? Did you learn from the conversations?
- Do you feel your understanding of the problem and the quality of the solution improved?
- Do you think the people you talked to are interested in learning how the project evolves?
- How would you characterize the conversations—boring, fun, exciting?

The 7 Principles

1. Personality matters less than skills you can learn.
2. The idea of a lifetime comes once a month.
3. Better than a great idea is an okay idea plus market feedback, flexibility, and iterations.
4. Start where you are with what you have.
5. Pitch and they'll judge. Ask advice and they'll help.
6. The problem leads to the solution.
7. Almost nothing inspires like helping others so much that they reward you for it.

UNIT 2

CREATING COMMUNITY

INTERLUDE
POLITE PERSISTENCE

A SKILL I alluded to in the last exercise that you will develop over the next few is *polite persistence*—among the most valuable skills in taking initiative. As the value of people you contact increases, reaching them usually, though not always, takes more effort, as does building the relationship. You'll find lulls in conversation. They get distracted. They don't respond as promptly. All sorts of complications.

That doesn't mean they won't appreciate your persisting through their resistance if you do it politely. The phrase "persistence pays off" stands the test of time for a reason. Persistence alone will overcome most obstacles. When your project is based on helping people, people you reach through persistence will appreciate your dedication to solving a meaningful problem, even if you help yourself in the process.

Some people worry that persisting too much will annoy others. Keeping your persistence polite and grounded in helping others will lead people to see you as mission-driven, in service of others, and therefore respectful and worthy of hearing out.

Some think of persisting as beneath them. I used to. I recommend thinking otherwise. Rarely do people, however important, disregard your reaching out for reasons personal to you, however much you may feel that they are. On the contrary, they rarely consider you at all if they don't know you. They're just busy.

Most of my podcast guests who are well known I booked by politely persisting, sometimes through many unanswered emails in a row. When I then book a Nobel Prize winner, Olympic gold medalist, or #1 bestselling author who thanks me for leading them to do a personal environmental challenge, it's worth it.

Even Seth Godin fans may not have recognized the title of the book I quoted him from in chapter 8. As of this writing, the only mention of it you'll find on Amazon is after a blurb for another author's book: "Seth Godin, author of *Footprints on the Moon*." Goodreads has several (shining) reviews, many saying how they got the book through Seth's altMBA program, which I didn't take. So how did I get the book?

Seth handed me a copy when I met him at his office. How did I meet him at his office? Because when he agreed to be a guest on my podcast, I politely persisted on recording in person, though online would have been easier. I took the train to meet him at his convenience. That's polite persistence.

10 Friends and Family Members

T HIS EXERCISE BUILDS on the last. It reinforces similar skills, experiences, and beliefs, while introducing new ones and developing your project more.

The exercise is to present your project to ten people and get three pieces of advice from each.

It does more than just develop your solution and help you understand the problem more. You'll develop new skills in starting conversations with less familiar people, coming up with people to talk to, and leading the conversations to build community.

You'll also continue to further develop the skills of presentation, soliciting advice, handling judgment, listening, and so on. Like in any performance-based activity, practice builds skills, experience, and beliefs.

As with the close contacts, we won't expect the best advice from this exercise. You'll get some useful advice and develop your project, but we're doing this mainly to develop skills, experiences, and beliefs for later exercises.

Action

1. List ten friends and family members likely to support you and unlikely to judge you. You'll probably have to include people less familiar than last time.

2. Schedule to meet with each in turn.
3. Tell each your project and get three pieces of advice from each.
4. Close each conversation by asking:
    i) "Is there anything to add that I didn't think to bring up?"
    ii) "Is there anyone you can think of you could put me in touch with who could help me with this?"
5. If you believe their advice will improve your project, implement it before presenting to the next person.

Begin the conversations similarly to the last exercise. Handle judgment, digressions, and so on with the skills you've developed. Describe the ideas conversationally, without slides—a sentence or two if possible.

Conversing by email doesn't count for this exercise either. You can schedule by email, and conversing by video or phone works if necessary, but meet ideally in person.

Nervous about contacting new people about your project? In the words of one former student, "I learned a lot this week, but most especially in taking initiative. Getting in touch with people is not as difficult and scary as it may seem. Stepping outside my comfort zone actually felt relatively comfortable when I just took initiative and did it. Starting a project from an idea is not something you have to wait around for a perfect opportunity to do. It can happen any time as long as you take initiative."

Deliverables

1. A list of **the advice you got** for your project.
2. An **improved version of the project** based on that advice.
3. A list of any **referrals** to people who could help.

I also recommend writing how the project developed. You could work from this template:

Old Problem: Sometimes people get caught in the rain and the cheap temporary umbrellas they have break.

Old Solution: Vending machines in subway stations with higher quality umbrellas, but more affordable by saving labor costs.

Advice 1:

Advice 2:

[...]

Advice 30:

New Problem: Same as old problem.

New Solution: Vending machines in convenience stores, safer than subways.

New Contacts: [*list of people referred to*]

Tips

You know the people you'll talk to, so you can start however you like, but in several future exercises you'll approach people you don't know. Practicing starting from cold now will prepare you, so, as with last time, I recommend scheduling the conversations with something like this tried-and-true opener:

> I'm working on a project for a class in entrepreneurship. I found a problem and came up with a solution. I think you could give useful advice on it. Do you mind if I tell it to you and ask for advice?

If they judge your idea instead of giving advice, I recommend patiently and politely responding with:

> I appreciate that you think it's a bad [or good, or however they judge it] idea. I'm really looking for advice. Can you give some advice on how I could improve the solution? Or to understand the problem better?

Most people are so used to judging that they judge without thinking. You'll develop conversational leadership skills by not responding to the judgment and steering them back to giving advice.

As with last exercise, you may also start to judge their advice without thinking. As with last time, practice responding with "thank you" to advice you don't like or can't use. You don't have to act on any advice. Even if you like their advice, I recommend not saying it's good since that still judges them, which will discourage many people from giving more advice.

Remember to end each conversation with:
1. Is there anything to add that I didn't think to bring up?
2. Is there anyone you can put me in touch with who could help me with this?

People close to you generally won't be able to offer great advice. You're developing experience by asking, handling responses, and seeing that most people like being asked—so that when you ask people in the field later, you'll be acting with experience and an expectation of success.

You'll be surprised by how often people bring up topics and people you wouldn't have thought of that end up helping you more than you would have expected.

A past student shared:

> One message I would like to pass on to the students taking this course next year is: be brave. Don't be afraid to be yelled at, or worry about others shutting the door on you. There is nothing to lose and even if there is little chance of people helping your project, you should open your mouth and talk to them. Also, try to get as much feedback or advice as possible. Maybe half of them are not useful at all, but surely you will find the gold in others' intelligence.

Another wrote:

> I, like many in the class, felt like I was asking a huge favor by asking people for feedback. But I found that people are really honored when we ask for their advice. It's essentially a huge compliment and they are (almost) always really excited to give you their feedback.

Checklist

☐ Did you talk to ten people?
☐ Did you get three pieces of advice from each?
☐ Did you finish each conversation with the two questions?
☐ Did you improve your project based on the advice?

Post-exercise Reflection

Before continuing, reinforce what you learned by reflecting. Put distractions away and spend a few minutes thinking about what you learned.

You can reflect on what you like, but here are some questions you might consider:

- How did you feel about the exercise before starting? Were you anxious, excited, confused?
- How did those feelings change as you did the exercise?
- How did you feel during the conversations? How did the other people seem to feel?
- Did you get advice beyond your expectations? Did you learn from the conversations?
- Do you feel your understanding of the problem and the quality of the solution improved?
- Do you think the people you talked to are interested in learning how the project evolves?
- How would you characterize the conversations—boring, fun, exciting?

The 7 Principles

1. Personality matters less than skills you can learn.
2. The idea of a lifetime comes once a month.

3. Better than a great idea is an okay idea plus market feedback, flexibility, and iterations.
4. Start where you are with what you have.
5. Pitch and they'll judge. Ask advice and they'll help.
6. The problem leads to the solution.
7. Almost nothing inspires like helping others so much that they reward you for it.

EXERCISE 5
5 People Who Feel the Problem

▓▓

THIS EXERCISE IS to find at least five people who feel the problem you are trying to solve, to talk to them about it, and to
express it in their words.

We've talked about understanding the problem. Most of us
consider problems from our perspectives. This exercise makes the
problem feel more *real* for most students. Many feel more sense of
purpose, even inspiration, the more deeply they hear and understand the problem from the place of someone feeling it. No matter
how well you feel you understand the problem, this exercise will
lead you to see and feel it in new, deeper, more visceral ways.

From an outreach perspective, knowing your customers' views
helps because their motivations motivate them, not yours or anyone else's. Many of their words will become sales copy, or some
equivalent for your project.

At this stage, though, feeling the problem from their place helps
you solve it. From an initiator's perspective, few things motivate like
understanding a problem as felt by the people it affects. You may also
hear people say, "How fast can you bring this out?" or "How soon
can I sign up?" or "Can I buy it already?"—which feels incredible.

An anonymous student review said:

> This class has pushed me to sit down with a stranger in Wash-
> ington Square Park and ask about their problems. I spent more
> time on phone calls than I would've ever imagined for one or two

pieces of advice. I have listened to random people I met tell me they would never be interested in my product. I have listened to random people I met ask me what my product is called so they can buy it. I have contacted people I would have never imagined (everyone from homeless people collecting plastic bottles to big executives thousands of miles away). And I have spent hours ranting to my parents about bank loans and calling up cousins to ask about marketing. This is nothing like the notes I thought I would be taking... It was much more beneficial to have the class set up this way as opposed to worksheets and tests. Hours trying condense my pitch in a classroom could never be as beneficial as being forced to pitch, answer questions, and ask for advice and feedback all before the subway doors opened at the next stop. I had to learn as I went along and I saw improvement (even over the course of very little time). Subsequent phone calls went more smoothly. Subsequent conversations were more productive. I could gather information more quickly as time went on because I began to learn where to look. I learned as I went because that was my only option and as a result, I found myself learning more in 20 minutes of talking to strangers than I would have in hours of reading a textbook.

Action

1. Find and talk to five people in the community you want to serve who feel the problem you want to solve. You may have to talk to more than five people to get meaningful quotes from five. Polite persistence helps.
2. Use your skills in leading and structuring the conversations to deflect judgment, deferring long digressions, and your other skills from past exercises. Talk to each about the problem. Listen to how it affects them and how they feel it. I recommend not trying to sell them on your solution, though you can if it comes up.
3. Write each person's problem in his or her words.

Deliverables

1. Five quotes, **one from each person you spoke with,** that states the problem in their terms from their perspective.

   If a conversation with one person feeling the problem doesn't lead to a quote, replace that person with another so you get at least five quotes.

   These statements should describe their emotion or the feeling they don't like in the situation you describe. Abstract statements like "people get caught in the rain without umbrellas" don't work.

   Statements like "John, a businessman, got caught in the rain and lost an important account by showing up late in a ruined, wet suit that a $5 umbrella could have prevented. He gets furious at himself when he talks about it" do.

Checklist

- [ ] Did you talk to five people feeling the problem?
- [ ] Did you write each description in their words?
- [ ] Can you describe the problem from their perspective in their words?
- [ ] Can you feel their problem better than before?

Post-exercise Reflection

Before continuing, reinforce what you learned by reflecting. Put distractions away and spend a few minutes thinking about what you learned.

You can reflect on what you like, but here are some questions you might consider:

- How did you feel about the exercise before starting? Were you anxious, excited, confused?
- How did your feelings change as you did the exercise?

- How did you feel during the conversations? How did the other people seem to feel?
- Do you feel differently about your project?
- Has your motivation changed?
- Do you feel your understanding of the problem and the quality of the solution improved?
- Do you think the people you talked to are interested in learning how the project evolves?
- How would you characterize the conversations—boring, fun, exciting?

The 7 Principles

1. Personality matters less than skills you can learn.
2. The idea of a lifetime comes once a month.
3. Better than a great idea is an okay idea plus market feedback, flexibility, and iterations.
4. Start where you are with what you have.
5. Pitch and they'll judge. Ask advice and they'll help.
6. The problem leads to the solution.
7. Almost nothing inspires like helping others so much that they reward you for it.

EXERCISE 6
10 People Closer to Your Field

JOANNE

Joanne did these exercises while pursuing a master's degree in engineering. Her project was to create a streaming channel for Broadway shows. As a Chinese citizen, her English was good but not fluent, giving her a double challenge for being both outside her professional field (though in her passion), and outside her native language and culture.

In class after doing exercise 6, I asked the students how it went, and Joanne shared her experience.

She wanted advice from a particular Broadway producer but didn't know how to reach him. Let's say his name was John. With no leads and nothing to lose, she called the ticket office of the theater, figuring they might know.

The ticket seller picked up. Joanne said she didn't want tickets but asked if they knew how to reach the producer. The ticket seller sounded annoyed and put her on hold.

Eventually, the line came back on and she heard: "Hello?" Only this time the voice sounded different. Joanne said, "Hello?"

The voice said, "Yes, this is John. Who is this?"

It was the producer!

Everyone in the class sat up at this surprise.

She told us how she couldn't think of what to do or say. She felt shocked and unprepared to talk to a valuable person so soon.

Only she *was* prepared. Having spoken to all those friends and family members, without thinking about it she said to him what she'd said to them: "I'm working on a project for a class in entrepreneurship. I saw a problem and came up with a solution. I think you could give useful advice on it. Do you mind if I tell it to you and ask for advice?"

Joanne told us that his response sounded like he nearly spat it out: "What is it?"

She described her project. *And he gave her advice.*

He got off the phone abruptly, so she described how flustered she felt. I suspect that she'd never cold called anyone before.

Seeing her anxiety, I asked her if her nerves settled afterward. She said yes. I asked if the project was ruined, if she regretted the experience, if the advice was worthless, and other questions that revealed her accomplishment from a practical perspective. As she answered and reflected, and she saw that no outcome more negative in the long run than her feeling flustered occurred, however unpleasant in the moment.

Her classmates looked riveted as I spoke to her. I pointed out how, from then on, she could honestly say that she had received support from a person everyone in the field would know. She could honestly say that he had helped develop the idea.

When her classmates saw how little they had to lose, they wanted to talk to such valuable people in their fields. If she could do it, so could they.

Joanne sat taller in her seat, her voice changing from timidity to pride. She began to wear the experience as a badge of honor.

Her experience led that class to begin a friendly competition to reach the most valuable person in their field. Though all engineers and non-native English speakers, for the remaining exercises, they approached people in their fields as enthusiastically as experienced salespeople.

This exercise builds on the one before last, only now you'll approach people outside your network and in your field.

This instruction—to repeat exercise 4 ("10 Friends and Family Members") with ten people closer to your project's field—may sound repetitive, but your new audience will develop in you new skills, experiences, and beliefs. We're still accessing them with the pattern that people like to hear entrepreneurial projects and give advice and feel motivated to help people they've advised.

This exercise will develop your project more than before. You'll become more a part of the communities relevant to your project. People in those communities will welcome you, support you, and connect you with their peers.

This exercise will lead valuable people you talk to in later exercises to see you as their peer. People you talk to in this exercise will connect you to those valuable people, creating warm introductions.

The exercise is to get advice from ten people, which may mean contacting more since not all will be available or will help you. You'll almost certainly have to persist politely. The additional challenge of identifying and contacting people until you get advice from ten will teach you new skills.

Your first challenge is to list people closer to your field of interest. The first three may be from your personal essay a few exercises ago. Earlier conversations may have gotten you several referrals.

Most students still have to think of more people beyond this low-hanging fruit. Many students have to overcome an internal block of thinking too narrowly of their fields and whom they can access.

Some perspectives that often help overcome that block:
- Of the more than seven billion people on the planet, there are plenty more than ten you can access, no matter the field.
- To make a music app, relevant fields may include app developers, app testers, musicians, non-musicians in the music business, people with a lot of music apps, and so on.
- You can meet many people in person. If your project relates to retail, you can walk into a relevant store and talk to a clerk or manager. For food-related projects, you might talk to a waiter, restaurant manager, food store manager, or the like. Most

students find that the people they talk to that way appreciate the break from their routine.

- Your second- and third-degree-of-separation contacts may number in the tens of thousands.
- You can call back people who gave you advice in earlier exercises and ask: "Is there anyone you can think of I could talk to who could help me with this?" or "Do you know anyone who might know people I could contact for advice on this project?"
- Warm referrals tend to be easier than cold calls. If contacting someone new makes you nervous, try to find a mutual contact to introduce you.
- You don't have to know all ten people before you start. You can get new contacts from conversations in this exercise.

I've given this exercise to hundreds of students and all have managed to finish it, many never having cold called before. You can too. Many had to do the exercise in New York City despite being foreigners here only for a year, not speaking English fluently. Many would describe themselves as introverted. All were as human as you.

However challenging they described it at first, they all loved the experience afterward for what it taught them.

Action

1. List as many people as you can that you can reach who are closer to your field.
2. Schedule to meet with several in turn.
3. Tell each about your project so far and get five pieces of advice from each.
4. Close each conversation with the following questions:
   i) "Is there anything to add that I didn't think to bring up?"
   ii) "Is there anyone you can think of I could talk to who could help me with this?"

5. If you believe the advice will improve your solution, implement it before presenting to the next person.
6. Repeat until you've gotten advice from ten people.

As in past exercises, describe the projects conversationally, without presentations or slides—a sentence or two if possible.

By email doesn't count for this exercise either. You can schedule by email, and converse by video or phone if necessary, but meet ideally in person.

An anonymous student evaluation said, "When I began contacting other people in the news industry I felt like I would be a nuisance to them, but instead people responded very positively and offered lots of feedback. Just by sending emails and making phone calls I was able to articulate better what I was trying to make and what kind of advice and help I needed."

Deliverables

1. A list of the **advice from ten people** relevant to your project.
2. An **improved version of the project** based on that advice.
3. A list of any **referrals** to people who could help.
4. **Your reflections** on the experience.

You could work from the same template as from exercise 4:

Old Problem: Sometimes people get caught in the rain and the cheap temporary umbrellas they have break.

Old Solution: Vending machines in subway stations with higher quality umbrellas, but more affordable by saving labor costs.

Advice 1:

Advice 2:

[…]

Advice 30:

New Problem: Same as old problem.

New Solution: Vending machines in convenience stores, safer than subways.

New Contacts: [*list of people referred to*]

Tips

Most people appreciate being contacted as a knowledgeable source of advice. Nearly all students find that most people they talk to in this exercise thank them. You did the hard part of initiating the conversation and making them feel like an expert. All they had to do was talk about their expertise.

Try for referrals to create warm connections instead of cold calls. If you introduce yourself by email, I recommend keeping the emails as short as you can while including enough to interest them.

Feel free to mention people and conversations from earlier exercises, especially when the person you're talking to knows them.

I recommend against describing yourself and the project in depth by email and then asking for advice in that email. Deciphering long emails asks too much and often results in short responses that close the connection. Instead, I recommend writing something like:

Hi [name],

I'm working on a project for a course in entrepreneurship and I'm looking for advice to improve my project. I came across [or, if a mutual acquaintance introduced you: so-and-so mentioned] your name as an expert in the field. I wonder if you'd be available for a call to answer a few short questions to give me advice.

Thank you,
[Your name]

Feel free to put it in your words while keeping the structure to what works.

If they judge your ideas instead of giving advice, use the techniques I introduced in exercise 3.

If you feel compelled to criticize or judge, practice saying "thank you." You don't have to act on anyone's advice.

End each conversation with:

1. Is there anything to add that I didn't think to bring up?
2. Is there anyone you can think of I could talk to who could help me with this?

Your skills and experience should lead more people to share contacts with you.

Checklist

- [ ] Did you get advice from (not just contact) ten people?
- [ ] Did you improve your project based on their advice?
- [ ] Did you close each conversation with the questions on leaving anything out and asking for referrals?

Post-exercise Reflection

Before continuing, reinforce what you learned by reflecting. Put distractions away and spend a few minutes thinking about what you learned.

You can reflect on what you like, but here are some questions you might consider:

- Is your understanding of the seven principles changing? If so, how?
- How did you feel about the exercise before starting? Were you anxious, excited, confused?

- How did your feelings change as you did the exercise?
- How did you feel during the conversations? How did the other people seem to feel?
- Did you get advice beyond your expectations? Did you learn from the conversations?
- Do you feel your understanding of the problem and the quality of the solution improved?
- Do you think the people you talked to are interested in learning how the project evolves?
- How would you characterize the conversations—boring, fun, exciting?

The 7 Principles

1. Personality matters less than skills you can learn.
2. The idea of a lifetime comes once a month.
3. Better than a great idea is an okay idea plus market feedback, flexibility, and iterations.
4. Start where you are with what you have.
5. Pitch and they'll judge. Ask advice and they'll help.
6. The problem leads to the solution.
7. Almost nothing inspires like helping others so much that they reward you for it.

INTERLUDE
PROFESSIONALIZING

BY THIS STAGE you:

- Understand the problem and solution.
- Can see the problem from the perspective of people who feel it.
- Have built a growing community of people who support you and feel personal success from your progress.

The next two exercises prepare you to get your project off the drawing board and into people's lives. You will refine the project you've spoken about conversationally to make it more sophisticated, professional, and viable. They will enable you to go from having an idea you casually talk about that gets interest from people you know—a remarkable achievement on its own—to speaking about it with successful, valuable decision-makers who can transition your project from the drawing board to a self-sustaining system that solves the problems of the people you serve, benefiting everyone involved.

Now that you've improved your project based on input from various sources, that transition probably doesn't seem so daunting. A project sustaining itself in the long term has to help everyone involved enough for each party to keep it going. The exercises so far have given you experience with getting their views so you could tailor the project to meet their needs to help them more.

Part of why I insist on speaking to a minimum number of people in the last exercise is to force you to expand your vision of your field from just the people you want to help to potential suppliers, employees, designers, developers, lawyers, people in government agencies, mentors, salespeople, and so on. If you can think of groups your project interacts with that you haven't spoken to, the skills, experiences, and beliefs should make talking to people from more groups natural.

I hope you've also seen the futility and counterproductivity of trying to develop ideas solo. Projects are social. Talking with the people your project interacts with develops that project. The idea of developing an idea for people you haven't talked about it with, expecting to spring it on the world fully formed, makes little sense from this perspective. You can't understand all its aspects, how other people benefit from it, or how they would benefit from it more without their suggestions.

Some businesses may be based on technology or other innovations they have to keep secret before launch, but even they have to work with suppliers, developers, and members of various communities. Every project benefits from talking to others. The question isn't if you talk to others, but how. Method Initiative's progression of exercises so far gives you the skills, experiences, and beliefs to answer for yourself.

You've probably also seen that your project will serve more than the people you intend to help. It serves all the relevant parties. For example, if your project is a for-profit company selling a physical product, you will serve your suppliers by meeting their needs to sell their inventory. You will serve your distributors who have their needs. You will serve your employees, the people who provide you professional services, and so on. If your project is a non-profit designed help an underserved group, you will serve your employees, your funding sources, your volunteers, and so on. If your project is a community organization, you will serve various groups.

Broadly speaking, having a long-term self-sustaining project means all relevant parties benefiting enough to reciprocate. So far you've refined what those groups are, what *benefit* means to them, and how to increase that benefit.

Ensuring that all of the groups relevant to the project benefit means thoughtful, empathetic organization. Ensuring they benefit enough requires quantification. The next two exercises will teach you to organize and quantify your project. In the process, you will refine the project and grow as a problem solver.

Nearly everyone sees the next two exercises as daunting before doing them, fun once they get into them, and transformative after they finish. You may struggle, but the outcome will be a sophisticated, professional understanding of your project that you will feel enthusiastic and excited to bring to valuable people you might have felt anxious or scared to approach before. You will also feel a deeper sense of ownership and inspiration for the project.

As with every stage, you may find that what worked so far might not pass the next stage. In this case, you may find the organization or numbers don't work out—that nothing you or anyone could do could make your project work. Even then, I predict the new skills, experiences, and beliefs that enabled you to discern the shortcomings you couldn't see or anticipate before will enable and compel you to restart with a new project, knowing that you'll be able to take it further than this one.

UNIT 3
REFINING YOUR SOLUTION

Create a Visual Model

T O GET YOUR project off the drawing board, we first have to put it on the drawing board. This exercise is to create a visual model of how your organization will operate and interact with others.

The exercise has two parts, each of which I'll outline step by step. In practice, you end up iterating—going back to earlier steps and refining them—so don't feel bad if you can't go straight through all the steps the first time. Few do. The process helps you learn about your project as part of professionalizing it.

Action

Step 1

List the people and groups that your organization will interact with, along with what they will give and receive through your project's operation.

Relevant people and groups may include individuals, or companies, government agencies, and more. Most lists include customers, suppliers, and employees. You can probably group into "professional services" landlords, accountants, lawyers, internet service providers, and the like.

What they give and receive depends on your project. Suppliers usually give materials and services in return for cash, but maybe you give them equity or advertising too. Employees usually give labor for cash, but maybe they get prestige or equity too.

Beware of your project involving a person or group only giving or only receiving. You may want to rework such areas to balance their relationships. At least explain why they would give or receive something for nothing. If you can't, you risk facing problems in that area. For example, if you are creating a non-profit and expect some employees to work as volunteers without receiving some value, you may risk high turnover.

The deliverable of step 1 is a three-column list like this, though yours would be more specific:

Person or Group	Gives	Gets
Me	Product (to buyers), money (to suppliers), etc.	Money (from buyers), supplies (from suppliers)
Supplier #1	Parts	Money
Supplier #2	Services	Money
Buyer #1	Money	My products
Employees	Labor	Money, equity

Step 2

This is the visual representation of your organization's operating model.

In the middle of a piece of paper, blackboard, computer screen, or wherever you can easily draw, write the name of your project (or "My organization" or "Me") and circle it.

Then, for each of the people and groups you listed in step 1, write their name in a circle.

Then, based on your list from step 1, draw arrows between each circle and every other circle that they interact with, labeling each arrow to show the operational relationships between them.

Say there is a hypothetical street produce vendor with an idea for a phone app that pre-sells produce as a way to get around the need for cash (an example inspired when I needed cash to buy from my local street produce vendor, and I figured he could sell more produce with non-cash payments). That hypothetical vendor also hires a marketer to drive sales. Here's how that visualization might look:

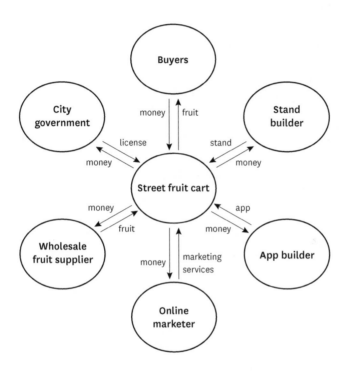

Note the modest level of detail. At this stage we aren't looking for perfection or polish for presentations to others. We are looking to refine our understanding and operating model.

Here is Chris's visual model, which resulted from many iterations and research:

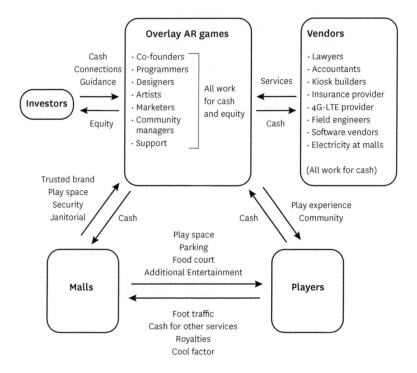

Here is one of Andreas's models and lists, showing a different style:

Name	Gives	Receives
Management companies / Tenant-owned apartments	Money	The bins & service
Production company	The bins	Money
Electrician	Installation electricity & internet	Money
ISP	Internet connection	Money
Web hosting company	Server	Money
Trash collector	Helps collecting trash from bins	Money
Employees	Labor	Money

Tips

Revise your list and diagram as much as you need to create a model that looks like it will work. Nearly everyone iterates several times until the list and diagram stabilize.

The goal for these deliverables is to develop your model and your entrepreneurial thinking, not to create polished presentations for investors, though it will lead to them.

Most students find this exercise quick and fun. Some find the exercise challenging but rewarding. It exposes potential problems they hadn't thought of. It leads them to understand their project in more detail and more holistically. It helps them think about and communicate their project. It also makes the next exercise easier.

This exercise will give you skills and fluency to express yourself visually in a natural way for structuring organizations.

Don't let their simplicity fool you into thinking making such diagrams is easy. As Steve Jobs said in a May 1998 interview with *Businessweek*: "Simple can be harder than complex: you have to work hard to get your thinking clean to make it simple. But it's worth it in the end because once you get there, you can move mountains."

Deliverables

1. A list of **your organization and the people and groups it will interact with,** including what each gives and receives. Explain or resolve any unmatched interactions.
2. A **visual model,** including each person or group from step 1 and an arrow for each flow of value.

Checklist

☐ Did you list all the people and groups you'll interact with?
☐ Did you balance all the arrows, or can you explain why anyone is giving or getting something for nothing?

Post-exercise Reflection

Before continuing, reinforce what you learned by reflecting. Put distractions away and spend a few minutes thinking about what you learned.

You can reflect on what you like, but here are some questions you might consider:

- Do you feel you understand your project's operations better now?
- How much did you revise your project during the exercise?
- Did you find potentially problematic areas? If so, what did you do about them?
- How did the exercise change your motivation to talk to others about your project?

The 7 Principles

1. Personality matters less than skills you can learn.
2. The idea of a lifetime comes once a month.
3. Better than a great idea is an okay idea plus market feedback, flexibility, and iterations.
4. Start where you are with what you have.
5. Pitch and they'll judge. Ask advice and they'll help.
6. The problem leads to the solution.
7. Almost nothing inspires like helping others so much that they reward you for it.

EXERCISE 8
Details, Sustainability, and Financials

THE FASHION-MODEL-TURNED-ENTREPRENEUR Rita's reflection bears repeating here: "This was such a fun exercise! It was so satisfying to have all the numbers mapped out like this. I feel I have a better handle on where to spend the money and where I can cut back. I found it amazing how lowering a cost even by $25 a month really affected the accumulated profit. I'm now motivated to talk with programmers and get a better idea of the cost and how I could save on this expense without losing quality."

We're nearly ready to talk to valuable people about our projects. If you talked to them based on your understanding before doing financials, you'd build relationships, but you'd lack the deep understanding and confidence of knowing the details of your project that this exercise gives.

This exercise is to create financial projections for your project. If financials scare you as much as they scared me when I started my first business, fear not. While professional accounting is essential for running many businesses, the initiator or entrepreneur doesn't need a professional at this stage. For most people outside of finance, too much professionalism would obscure more than reveal. Few successful projects began with professional financials.

Financials exist for a reason. They reveal operational details like nothing else. Creating them forces you to learn your operations to a level that will make valuable people in the field take you seriously.

Method Initiative has you create a simplified, effective version of financials that everyone so far has been able to do. They've enjoyed it, including initially scared teenagers who had never used a spreadsheet, business school students, and experienced working professionals.

Our goal is not to create polished, professional financials to present to investors. Our goal with our simplified financials is twofold:

1. To learn the operational **details and assumptions** as only financials reveal.
2. To ensure the organization will operate **viably and sustainably.**

Why financials?

Financials for organizations are like a patient's vital statistics to a medical doctor. You wouldn't want a doctor to treat you without knowing your pulse, blood pressure, and so on. He or she might go on wild goose chases or miss something important without them. Likewise, talking to valuable people in your field or planning your project without knowing how to organize it can lead to similar wild goose chases.

Vital statistics versus a personal trainer

You need a doctor if you want to check for disease or to fix a broken bone, but to get in shape, a personal trainer or coach may help more. A trainer's knowledge may be more practical and functional. A trainer may motivate you more. A trainer may be able simply to look at you or have you try a few activities to guide you.

The initiator's goal is often closer to getting fit than diagnosing a disease. Method Initiative's financials are like a coach or personal trainer. They don't go into as much depth, but they are functional and practical. Just as a mature person will go to a doctor more with age, as your project matures, you'll benefit more from professional financials and risk more if you ignore them, so you can't rely on this exercise forever.

But I don't need financials

Maybe you're creating a community organization, a book club, or some project that doesn't involve money flowing.

Even so, you will almost certainly benefit from finding a way to quantify in dollars the flow of value, which may come through time, labor, physical goods, or other exchange, and still do this exercise. In the hundreds of projects I've seen go through this exercise, maybe a dozen or so suggested they didn't need to or couldn't do financials. All of them ultimately found ways to quantify their projects' flow of value and, after doing the exercise, found the exercise more than worth their time and effort.

Beyond figuring out their projects' details, assumptions, and sustainability, they developed the skills, experiences, and beliefs in understanding an organization through accounting and financials. Accounting has stood the test of time to understand and manage organizations for centuries for a reason—not because it's fun, though many have found this exercise fun, but because it works.

Simple, Effective Method Initiative (SEMI) financials

The financials for this exercise are simplified relative to what bankers and financiers do. Following these instructions in an accounting or finance class would probably get you failed. They include enough to force you to understand your organization and determine its viability and sustainability.

So please don't confuse SEMI financials for professional ones, which isn't the goal of this exercise.

You can use even SEMI financials to go into depth. In Chris's case, they led him to "massive revisions," deep understanding, and attracting teammates, likely because of the professionalism they showed about him and his project. He said:

> The exercise forced me to do a lot of research into costs of team personnel, vendors, and venues (malls). I had to speak to about two dozen people to do this and have about 40 pages of notes referencing the numbers in the spreadsheet...

Each iteration had problem areas that were a result of dubious assumptions on my part. These dubious assumptions were almost always a case of being overly optimistic about the amount of staff needed or the amount of time needed to accomplish different tasks. I was pretty good at estimating costs for salaries and vendors but needed to build in more people and more time. I also had to halve the assumption about average monthly ticket sales per venue.

The result of the process was that each successive pro forma created a flatter, less dramatic hockey stick. However, it still creates a very nice return over 48 months...

The exercise forced me to speak with lots of others. Those conversations led to recruiting a great team of programmers and business partners interested in taking the concept to investors.

A personal aside

One summer, at an NYU dean's request, I taught these exercises in a high school summer program. The program is designed to give students a university experience, and, for foreign students, an American experience.

The challenge was that I had to teach the course block-week style—that is, we had to cover the full 14-week course in one week, Monday to Friday, 9 a.m. to 5 p.m. This exercise was particularly challenging, since most of the students had never done financials and many had never used a spreadsheet.

I prepared them as I'll prepare you in this exercise. The time constraints of the program allowed them two hours to do steps 3 through 5 in the classroom. Two hours is a challenge for anyone, let alone students using spreadsheets for the first time; but rather than being impossible, doing it quick-and-dirty develops different skills. Chris, for comparison, took months to create his financials, but he used the exercise to learn his business in more detail and create relationships with people in the field.

After I walked my students through setting up their pages in steps 1 and 2, they started working. The room fell silent.

About an hour later, one student raised her hand and asked, "Do we have to pay our employees the new minimum wage or can we pay them the old one?"

That summer, headlines covered New York State raising its minimum wage to $15 per hour, but the measure hadn't passed yet.

I asked the student to clarify.

She said, "I can make the numbers work if I pay my employees the old minimum wage but not the new one."

Another student said, "Same here. If I have to pay them $15 an hour I can't hire them at all."

Without my prompting, the class began discussing the effects of raising the minimum wage. They didn't debate it. They talked about how it affected their businesses, as well as society in general.

I suspect that had I asked them their thoughts on the minimum wage law, nearly all would have supported it, since high school students tend to earn minimum wage. Instead, I witnessed a calm, productive conversation exposing several views such as "Isn't $11 an hour better than nothing?" and "If you can't pay them enough, should your business be allowed to run?" and "What else can you do to make it work?"

It was a dream experience as an educator, since my goal isn't to give them answers but to give them the tools to find out what to ask and how to answer. It reinforced the value of project-based learning so their work isn't sterile and academic. They helped each other understand and solve each other's problems.

I let them explore the issue for a while. Then I proposed the following: "Say the measure passes and you have to pay $15 an hour. Are there ways you can motivate and pay your employees besides with money?"

On their own, they started coming up with options like performance-based pay and paying in part with equity.

At the end of the two hours, all the students finished usable financials and had learned some of their projects' key assumptions, as best I could tell. The financials weren't professionally laid out, but they got the idea.

Action

If you have experience making profit and loss statements, feel free to make them how you know. If not, the following five steps will show you how to make SEMI financials.

With your visual model from last exercise in front of you, open a spreadsheet. Plenty of free spreadsheet programs exist (I use LibreOffice). I'll illustrate with my model from the last exercise— an app for a produce stand that lets people pre-order and avoid using cash.

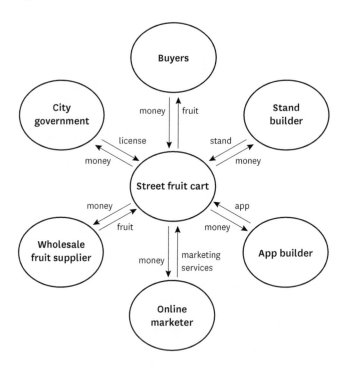

Step 1
Make the structure of the spreadsheet. First, write the word "Month" in a cell near the top left, and then 1 through 24 in the cells across the top, like this:

A	B	C	D	E	F	G	H		W	X	Y
Month	1	2	3	4	5	6	7		22	23	24

In the left column, put the terms "Revenues," "Total Revenues," "Costs," "Total Costs," "Profit," and "Cumulative Profit," in bold with a few rows between, like this:

A	B	C	D	E	F	G	H		W	X	Y
Month	1	2	3	4	5	6	7		22	23	24
Revenues											
Total Revenues											
Costs											
Total costs											
Profit											
Cumulative Profit											

Step 2

Enter your left column entries. On your visual model, your organization has arrows in and out. For each arrow in that corresponds to money, put an entry under "Revenues" (note that some arrows in may not be revenues, like investment, so we're simplifying). For each arrow out that corresponds to money, put an entry under "Costs." (Again, some may not be actual financial costs; we're simplifying.)

A	B	C	D	E	F	G	H		W	X	Y
Month	1	2	3	4	5	6	7		22	23	24
Revenues											
Fruit sold (cash)											
Fruit sold (app)											
Total Revenues											
Costs											
City license (annual)											
Fruit stand											
Salary											
Cost to build app											
Cost to market app											
Wholesale fruit to sell											
Total costs											
Profit											
Cumulative Profit											

You may have to adjust the rows. I added a row for "Salary," which wasn't on the visual model, and I split the revenues into fruit sold by cash and by app.

The financials, the visual model, and the list from the last exercise combine into an iterative cycle leading to more deeply understanding and often refining your project, preparing you for running it and presenting it to others. Starting with a visual model makes making the financials easier, as Chris found when he had made his financials first:

In retrospect, doing [Create a Visual Model] before doing [SEMI financials] would be a much more efficient sequence to get a complete picture of what the business needs. In the way it worked out this time my diagram is a reflection of my pro forma doc. In the future it will be more efficient to make the diagram first and then make the pro forma as a reflection of the diagram.

Step 3

Fill in the numbers for your monthly revenues and costs. Enter dollar numbers for the rows you labeled in step 2. You will have to assume. A main goal of this exercise is to learn your assumptions, so remember the assumptions that make the biggest differences. Those assumptions will become the foundations of your strategy. Valuable people will ask about this in exercise 10.

For example, say you love cooking and want to start a restaurant. Absent this exercise, you might focus mainly on recipes, decor, and other visible parts of a restaurant. Financials will lead people in most cities to assume a lot around rent and salaries, suggesting that rent and salaries are important parts of your business worth focusing your attention on.

Here is a middle step of Step 3, where I entered the Month 1 numbers, as well as the later months where they change from Month 1:

A	B	C	D	E	F	G	H		W	X	Y
Month	1	2	3	4	5	6	7		22	23	24
Revenues											
Fruit sold (cash)	500	500	500	500	500	500	500		500	500	500
Fruit sold (app)	100	120	140	160	180	200	220		520	540	560
Total Revenues											
Costs											
City license (annual)	5,000										
Fruit stand	10,000										
Salary	1,500										
Cost to build app	4,000										
Cost to market app	50										
Wholesale fruit to sell	300										
Total costs											
Profit											
Cumulative Profit											

Here I filled in the numbers for all the months:

A	B	C	D	E	F	G	H		W	X	Y
Month	1	2	3	4	5	6	7		22	23	24
Revenues											
Fruit sold (cash)	500	500	500	500	500	500	500		500	500	500
Fruit sold (app)	100	120	140	160	180	200	220		520	540	560
Total Revenues											
Costs											
City license (annual)	5,000	0	0	0	0	0	0		0	0	0
Fruit stand	10,000	0	0	0	0	0	0		0	0	0
Salary	1,500	1,500	1,500	1,500	1,500	1,500	1,500		1,500	1,500	1,500
Cost to build app	4,000	0	0	0	0	0	0		0	0	0
Cost to market app	50	50	50	50	50	50	50		50	50	50
Wholesale fruit to sell	300	310	320	330	340	350	360		510	520	530
Total costs											
Profit											
Cumulative Profit											

Step 4

Calculate the totals. To do so, put formulas into the bold rows you created in step 1. I'll leave it to you to find how to do them, since the internet has many resources for creating formulas in spreadsheets. Briefly:

- Total Revenues is the sum of all revenues.
- Total Costs is the sum of all costs.
- Profit is Total Revenues minus Total Costs.
- Cumulative Profit is last month's Cumulative Profit plus this month's Profit.

Here's how this looks:

A	B	C	D	E	F	G	H	W	X	Y
Month	1	2	3	4	5	6	7	22	23	24
Revenues										
Fruit sold (cash)	500	500	500	500	500	500	500	500	500	500
Fruit sold (app)	100	120	140	160	180	200	220	520	540	560
Total Revenues	**600**	**620**	**640**	**660**	**680**	**700**	**720**	**1,020**	**1,040**	**1,060**
Costs										
City license (annual)	5,000	0	0	0	0	0	0	0	0	0
Fruit stand	10,000	0	0	0	0	0	0	0	0	0
Salary	1,500	1,500	1,500	1,500	1,500	1,500	1,500	1,500	1,500	1,500
Cost to build app	4,000	0	0	0	0	0	0	0	0	0
Cost to market app	50	50	50	50	50	50	50	50	50	50
Wholesale fruit to sell	300	310	320	330	340	350	360	510	520	530
Total costs	**28,050**	**1,860**	**1,870**	**1,880**	**1,890**	**1,900**	**1,910**	**2,060**	**2,070**	**2,080**
Profit	**-20,250**	**-1,240**	**-1,230**	**-1,220**	**-1,210**	**-1,200**	**-1,190**	**-1,040**	**-1,030**	**-1,020**
Cumulative Profit	**-20,250**	-21,490	-22,720	-23,940	-25,150	-26,350	-27,540	-49,190	-50,220	-51,240

Uh oh, something looks wrong.

My financials show I'll lose money every month, which isn't sustainable.

It's not wrong. It's part of the process. Most people find similar results with their first financials. Unsuccessful would-be initiators might give up at this point, but we won't.

Why not? Almost no first financial projection works. Projecting something new means we don't know the best way to do it and our first way will rarely be best. We're also assuming a lot, motivated by enthusiasm and optimism, which means we probably haven't figured out all the revenues we could create and all the costs we could cut.

In my example, I know produce stands make money. My assumptions suggest that regular produce stands wouldn't work, but they do—so I probably assumed wrong.

The next step resolves the problem and transforms you from a dreamer to someone who is a step closer to being a successful initiator.

Step 5
Adjust the numbers until the project doesn't lose money, keeping in mind how adjusting the numbers affects your project's operations. Most students and clients at this stage need to increase revenues, decrease costs, or both. Sometimes they have to change the structure in the visual model.

Remember in high school science lab when you measured something and didn't get the results you were supposed to "discover"—so you adjusted your measurement numbers to look "right"?

In science you aren't supposed to change the data. In initiating a project, you *can* change the numbers. In fact, you should—*as long as you propagate how those changes affect your organization and its operations.*

If you raise sales, for example, you may have to work harder for them. Can you? You may have to hire another salesperson or pay a marketing company. If so, include the new costs.

Likewise, lowering your costs may result in lower revenues, a rise in other costs (like maintenance), or higher turnover. If you can't lower costs, sometimes you can delay them, which often helps.

Many initiators go without salaries while starting their projects. If your bank account were to drop, would you risk losing your home? Would you be able to work effectively, or would you start looking for a job?

Many questions that arise in this step will force deep thinking and lead you to ask people with more experience for advice. You will grow as an initiator, person, and citizen. You'll probably enjoy the conversations and how they develop your skills, experiences, and beliefs.

Nearly everyone has to adjust their financial assumptions. Most have to adjust their visual models. Some have to reexamine whom they're serving or what problem they're solving. Many will restart from exercise 1, this time understanding themselves and the initiating process more accurately. As with changing projects, they catch back up in a fraction of the first time, and they enjoy the process more.

In an example like a restaurant, if your assumptions show it can't work—great! You know restaurants can work, so you know you have to learn something about your field. Better to learn now than after you spend money on it or leave your current job.

If you work in a company and want to create a project to gain responsibility or a promotion, finding out what you need to make your project work may lead you to build relationships, knowledge, and skills that lead decision-makers to promote you even if you don't start your project—*even before you propose it*. Rafael did.

People often start getting job offers during this exercise.

Back to my produce stand: I resolved my problem by increasing some revenues and decreasing some costs, resulting in profitability in month 24. It's not a particularly profitable business yet, but if sales through the app keep increasing and I can use the same app for a chain of produce stands, the overall business could become profitable. Here's what the spreadsheet looked like:

A	B	C	D	E	F	G	H	W	X	Y
Month	1	2	3	4	5	6	7	22	23	24
Revenues										
Fruit sold (cash)	700	700	700	700	700	700	700	700	700	700
Fruit sold (app)	200	300	400	500	600	700	800	2,300	2,400	2,500
Total Revenues	**900**	**1,000**	**1,100**	**1,200**	**1,300**	**1,400**	**1,500**	**3,000**	**3,100**	**3,200**
Costs										
City license (annual)	5,000	0	0	0	0	0	0	0	0	0
Fruit stand	7,500	0	0	0	0	0	0	0	0	0
Salary	1,500	1,500	1,500	1,500	1,500	1,500	1,500	1,500	1,500	1,500
Cost to build app	4,000	0	0	0	0	0	0	0	0	0
Cost to market app	50	50	50	50	50	50	50	50	50	50
Wholesale fruit to sell	450	500	550	600	650	700	750	1,500	1,550	1,600
Total costs	**18,500**	**2,050**	**2,100**	**2,150**	**2,200**	**2,250**	**2,300**	**3,050**	**3,100**	**3,150**
Profit	**-17,600**	**-1,050**	**-1,000**	**-950**	**-900**	**-850**	**-800**	**-50**	**0**	**50**
Cumulative Profit	-17,600	-18,650	-19,650	-20,600	-21,500	-23,150		-34,150	-34,150	-34,100

For those more familiar with spreadsheets, I made a more thorough result, beyond what's necessary for this exercise—though still SEMI—that shows more assumptions, formulas, and more. It's available at joshuaspodek.com/initiative-downloads.

This exercise does not prepare you to present financials to others, which is beyond its scope of this exercise, but it gets you a lot closer.

Deliverables

1. A **spreadsheet** in which the number in the Profit row becomes positive by the last month.

Beside your spreadsheet, describe what you consider important in the project (typically the main revenues and costs), your main assumptions, how long it takes to become profitable, what investment or loan you'll need, what you consider the biggest challenges, what you had to change the most, and any other thoughts that seem relevant.

Checklist

☐ Did you follow all the steps in the Action section?

☐ Did you keep track of and understand all of the project's important assumptions?

☐ Did you find a way for your project to reach sustainability within a time appropriate to you?

☐ Did you figure out your rough investment needs, if any, and do you feel comfortable with them?

☐ Do you remember that SEMI financials aren't designed for presenting to professionals?

Post-exercise Reflection

Before continuing, reinforce what you learned by reflecting. Put distractions away and spend a few minutes thinking about what you learned.

You can reflect on what you like, but here are some questions you might consider:

- Do you feel you understand your project's operations better now?
- How much did you revise your project during the exercise?
- Did you find potentially problematic areas? If so, what did you do about them?
- How did the exercise change your motivation to talk to others about your project?

The 7 Principles

1. Personality matters less than skills you can learn.
2. The idea of a lifetime comes once a month.
3. Better than a great idea is an okay idea plus market feedback, flexibility, and iterations.
4. Start where you are with what you have.
5. Pitch and they'll judge. Ask advice and they'll help.
6. The problem leads to the solution.
7. Almost nothing inspires like helping others so much that they reward you for it.

CREATING PROFESSIONAL RELATIONSHIPS WITH VALUABLE PEOPLE

Second Personal Essay

T HIS EXERCISE IS to write a second personal essay.

You already wrote a personal essay. Why a second?

I used to assign people to talk to valuable people after they finished the financials in exercise 8, but I found they didn't act as confidently and assertively as their new skills, experiences, and beliefs warranted. They didn't see how much progress they had made, particularly in their status in their fields.

You've developed a project that may not have existed before, and improved it based on advice from dozens, including people in the field. They've likely referred you to others in the field, whom you can approach as warm contacts. If you switched projects, you've developed skills, experiences, and beliefs from multiple approaches, likely reinforcing each other.

You've probably heard people with the problem ask how soon your project would be ready. People probably see you as one who takes initiative and responsibility.

I've found it helpful to reflect on your development. Your project may not have existed and you may have felt inexperienced a few weeks or months ago, but that was then. Now if you expect your project to help people and that you can make it happen, others don't have to know that the old you might have felt insecure.

Writing a second personal essay helps you see your overall progress, which will build your confidence, motivation, comfort, and expectation of success, along with a sense of belonging in the community that will lead to more productive conversations with others in that field.

Action

Write a personal essay about yourself in relation to:
- The seven principles
- Your field of interest
- The problem you want to solve
- The people who feel the problem
- Your solution and goals
- Taking initiative in general
- Your motivation and, I hope, inspiration and purpose

You may want to refer to your experiences and results from the exercises so far, including:

- The people you've talked to who feel the problem
- The people you've talked to in the field
- The relationships you've formed in these areas, especially if they've become productive and mutually beneficial
- The advice you've received
- The advice you've acted on
- The depth of your understanding of the problem and solution, including the model and financials
- The depth of your understanding what this problem and solution mean to you

You may also want to discuss your plans for your project, your role in it, roles for others, and so on.

Most students write longer essays for their second ones. I recommend at least 1,000 words, but write whatever amount sets a foundation of your understanding of your project and of motivation to talk to and collaborate with valuable people in your field.

Checklist

☐ Did you sleep on what you wrote and edit it after?
☐ Did you write in a way that's easy for others to read and understand?

Post-exercise Reflection

Before continuing, reinforce what you learned by reflecting. Put distractions away and spend a few minutes thinking about what you learned.

You can reflect on what you like, but here are some questions you might consider:

• Did you learn anything about yourself in writing the essay?
• Do you feel you changed more, less, or about the same as you expected before writing?
• How do you feel about:
  • Responsibility?
  • Motivation?
  • Initiative?
  • Entrepreneurship?
• What do you feel has been most meaningful, valuable, important, or purposeful about your project so far? Or your personal development?

The 7 Principles

1. Personality matters less than skills you can learn.
2. The idea of a lifetime comes once a month.
3. Better than a great idea is an okay idea plus market feedback, flexibility, and iterations.
4. Start where you are with what you have.

5. Pitch and they'll judge. Ask advice and they'll help.
6. The problem leads to the solution.
7. Almost nothing inspires like helping others so much that they reward you for it.

INTERLUDE
HOW TO PROMPT
JOB OFFERS AND
HOW TO RESPOND

MOST RESOURCES ON entrepreneurship celebrate it as the antithesis of jobs, which they present as a lamentable outcome for uncreative types. Yet many people love their jobs. They find them sources of freedom and opportunity.

Whether you work for yourself or for others, what creates meaning at work is the emotions you feel about your work. Does it bring you more joy, challenge, and optimism, or more drudgery, compliance, and pessimism? People love having a sense of ownership of their work—responsibility, a say in the outcome, accountability, passion for the results, and so on.

More fundamental to your relationship with what you do is your ability to create that relationship.

A skilled boss can give you that sense of ownership in a job. An overbearing investor can take it away in a venture you founded. But the best way I know to create and keep that sense of ownership is by creating the project, or by leading decision-makers to delegate it to you—in short, to create the terms of your relationship with what you do.

Initiators create those terms. I avoided titling this book *Entrepreneurship* partly because people associate it with Dog Show Entrepreneurship, but also because starting a venture is only one way to get the benefits of creating the terms of your work.

If you work in a firm now, you can create as much joy, challenge, and optimism by creating a project within it, or by getting promoted, or getting hired in a new firm. Because Method Initiative projects are grounded in helping others, you'll get the same satisfaction of making the world a better place.

People with Resources Hire and Promote Initiators

When decision-makers see you building constructive relationships and solving problems, they want you on their teams, meaning they want to hire you. If they know you can solve problems, they won't want you solving small ones. They'll want you solving big ones. So seeing you solve problems motivates them to promote you.

Wanting to hire and promote you doesn't mean that they'll overtly *offer* you jobs and promotions. On the contrary, they tend to hide opportunities. As with creating projects, your skills, experiences, and beliefs will make things happen.

Why They Hide Opportunities

People with resources don't publicize their best opportunities, nor do they explicitly offer chances to act on them, even when people acting on them would help them.

Why not?

Let's look at three top reasons.

First, people approach them all the time to access their resources. As a result, most develop filters against people wasting those resources or their time. They don't know whom they can trust. Common defenses include "Talk to HR," "Talk to my assistant," "That's interesting, write a proposal," and "Let's look at it again next quarter when we have a new budget." Maybe you've hit these defenses.

Second, even a solution they expect to work takes time and other resources to start. It could fail, go over budget, take too long, and hit other snags.

Third, exposing their problems makes them vulnerable, whether the problem is business or personal. We all protect our vulnerabilities and a top way to is to hide them. Sometimes they aren't consciously aware themselves of their problems.

How to Create Opportunities

Creating opportunities means prompting them to offer roles you can fill.

Method Initiative's approach in its early exercises of seeking advice and building connections from the outside in helps get past many filters. While nobody can reach everyone on their first try, you'll reach several valuable people that way. The more you meet and keep them updated on how you respond to their advice, the more they'll introduce you to others, and the more those new people will receive you as a member of their community.

Focusing on a project a person can support with just a few words of advice often overcomes their need to protect their time and resources. They can enjoy your success vicariously, which motivates them to stay involved.

You address the issue of vulnerability by listening and maintaining the relationship. The more they see you as a problem solver, the more they will share their problems with you.

There is a technical term in business for when a person with resources tells you their problems. I ask my in-person classes every year if they know the technical term. So far, no one has.

The technical term for when a person with resources tells you their problems is a *job offer*.

The person with the problem might not recognize it as an offer when they say it, nor might you when you hear it. Week after week

I told Andreas that job offers—in the form of people sharing their problems with him—would come from connecting with and asking advice from those in the field. He kept saying it never happened.

One week he happily reported getting his first job offer and I coached him on how to respond.

The following week he said, "Wow, people have been offering me jobs the whole time. I never realized it." Knowing how to respond and to experience responding increases your sensitivity to the subtleties of how they open the door.

Seeing you as someone who solves problems and is not seeking their resources leads people to share their problems with you. Why wouldn't they? If you're good at solving problems selflessly, viably, and sustainably, *you might solve theirs and improve their lives.* Method Initiative leads you to make it in their interests to share.

Common ways people voice opportunities include:
- You're talking about design work necessary for your project and in passing they say, "... we haven't been able to find someone to do that..."
- They're giving you advice and say, "... we should do that here too..."
- Or you might hear, "... we tried it and it didn't work, but it should..."

The key is to listen, putting their interests first. Listening from their perspective is hard at first, especially when focusing on your project. It comes with practice and experience—especially after your first time converting their sharing a problem into your proposing a solution.

How to Respond to an Opportunity

Your response is what turns their problem statement into a job offer. I can't guarantee that these responses will always work, but they often will, and I've never heard that one hurt.

What I call the magic phrases are:

- "I'm experienced at it."
- "I'm good at it."
- "I like doing it."

You can use variations and you don't have to say them all in one sentence, but conveying their meaning will get many people thinking about using you to solve their problem. For example, when someone mentions being unable to find designers, if you wanted to work with that person, you might say, "You know, I helped a couple of companies find some great designers. I'm good at finding and vetting them. I guess it's because I like working with people from that community."

If you're a designer yourself—or in whatever role someone you're talking to is looking for—you might say: "Design? I have a lot of experience in design. People tell me they like my work. I like that kind of work."

You don't have to say much more to motivate their thinking about you as a possible solution. I recommend not saying more because trying to sell yourself too early, such as adding, "Let me tell you about some projects I worked on," or telling them how good you are, will motivate them to start evaluating you or raising their defenses.

If they show interest, it's still not the time to start selling yourself. Instead, ask them to clarify their problem. If you've practiced Method Initiative so far and they see you as a problem solver, they'll expand. At this point, ask clarification questions and resist pitching yourself. Building a productive relationship where you support them for sharing problems—rather than take advantage of them—prompts the most offers.

Naturally, if you have no relevant experience, aren't skilled at it, or don't like the work, faking this tactic will ultimately hurt your relationship. Note, however, that you can solve their problem multiple ways. If you aren't skilled in design, for example, you might still be skilled in finding designers.

If they continue sharing, and if solving the problem continues to sound attractive, *then* the door is open to start proposing yourself. I still recommend giving yourself a chance to create more compelling solutions than you can come up with in the moment. I also recommend continuing to build the relationship, over merely furthering your personal interests.

Here's something you can say to continue the relationship:

> I have a couple beginnings of ideas for what you're talking about. If you give me a week to develop them, could I share what I come up with with you?

I use the following variation:

> I have a couple half-baked ideas for what you're talking about. If you give me a week to fully bake them, could I share what I come up with with you?

I think it sounds more innocent. Speak consistently with your personality and your relationship to the person you're talking to.

Then use the week you asked for to figure out how to propose a collaboration. You don't need to solve their problem, only to show how promoting or hiring you will enable you to solve it.

If their problem doesn't connect to your project, you may have to create a solution to their problem. Does that sound hard? It shouldn't, because in your hands is a book that describes how to create solutions to problems. You now have a week, or however long you asked for, to apply this book's exercises to that person's problem.

Whether you adapt your current project or develop a new one, once they tell you they're open to a fully baked plan, start scheduling conversations with close supportive friends, then friends and family, and so on through Method Initiative's steps. You'll find yourself running through the exercises faster and more enthusiastically with a deadline and a person to deliver your results to.

Generalizing

Again, this technique won't work every time, usually for reasons beyond your control or knowledge, and the first few times you do it, you'll flail like a sprinting child. But each time, you'll do it more naturally. You'll pick up more subtle cues. You'll listen more and see it from their perspective more, which will allow you to propose more helpful solutions and build the relationship more, which will result in their sharing more opportunities and connections to others.

Experience will lead you to hear "job offers" in more relationships, especially with people who have authority over you. You'll look forward to hearing valuable people complain because you'll know how to distill opportunity from the complaints. Even problems from people without resources may point you to people *with* resources who you can follow up with.

A Review

Here's a quick review on how to prompt job offers:
- Offers may come in any stage, but more often in later exercises, when your project is more developed and the people more valuable.
- Present yourself as a problem solver interested in solving problems relevant to their communities—that is, practice Method Initiative.
- Listen for people to share their problems.
- When a problem interests you, respond with the magic phrases: "I'm experienced at it," "I'm good at it," and "I like doing it."
- Ask for time to prepare a fully baked idea.
- Use that time to use this book's processes on their problem.
- Propose it to them.

EXERCISE 10
Valuable People

―――――――――――――

THIS EXERCISE CULMINATES everything we've done so far. You'll practice the same skills you have been learning in the previous exercises, with people who can help you more.

This exercise is to repeat exercise 4 ("10 Friends and Family Members") and exercise 6 ("10 People Closer to Your Field") but with ten valuable people.

A few conversations in which you get advice from valuable people will establish you as an important member of that community. They may offer to fund your project, hire you for an internal project, or just agree to meet with you. You can share these signs of relationships with other valuable people.

This exercise delivers more value to nearly all projects than preparing for *Shark Tank*, a business plan competition, or nearly any spectacle from Dog Show Entrepreneurship. Instead of delivering elevator pitches prompting people who may only tangentially know or care about your field to judge you, you'll actively and deliberately create connections with people you choose. Instead of them seeing you as a commodity lucky to pitch them, they'll see you as a peer and problem solver.

An anonymous student review said, "If you had told me coming into this week that I would have a 15-minute conversation over the phone with a CEO of a large advertising firm I wouldn't believe you. However, through the skills and phone calls that I placed

I was able to do just that, and also gain very valuable information on possible business ideas."

Value

First, what do we mean by "valuable"?

Value, in this context, means that they can help your project. Your problem and solution are unique, so only you know how a person can help you.

Some things that make someone helpful include:

- Status
- Skills
- Connections
- Resources
- Experience
- Reputation
- Ability to motivate
- Having solved similar problems before
- Understanding
- Feeling the problem

Your first challenge is to think of such people. The first three may be from your first personal essay. Earlier exercises may have led people to give you connections.

Many students have to think hard about what people they could contact who could help them. Many recontact people they spoke to in past exercises to ask for new referrals. An effective way to recontact someone is to tell them you want to update them, especially if you used their advice. Even if you didn't, telling them you considered using it will warm most of them enough to talk more, which opens them to giving you referrals. If anyone has updated you on how they acted on advice you gave them, you know how good it feels, so you can expect them to welcome your update.

It may help to expand what areas you're looking for people in. If you're making a music app for phones, communities you might draw from include:
- App developers
- Musicians
- Heavy app users
- Creators of other music apps
- Creators of other apps
- Designers
- Investors in similar apps
- Investors in music companies
- Teachers of app development, music, or entrepreneurship
- App reviewers
- Music reviewers

I could add more. Most students find that they can find more places for help and connections to valuable people after some reflection.

Despite having developed a strong command of their project and community, some students still feel nervous talking to valuable people who could potentially make or break their projects. If you feel confident, great! You can skip this section. For others, here are some perspectives that often help overcome inhibitions:

- Think about the problem you want to solve and the people it affects. You are helping them. You are acting in service of others.
- You probably contacted and spoke to more people than you dreamed of before these exercises.
- Of over seven billion people on the planet, you can access lot more than ten who can help in some way.
- Like Joanne and the producer who advised her, you can create social proof by talking about conversations you've had with others in the field and how they've contributed to your solution. You won't be gratuitously name-dropping because you had genuine conversations and acted on their advice.

- People who can help can come from many areas, including potential investors, potential employees, other entrepreneurs, and so on.
- People like helping others solve problems that affect their communities, especially when someone else does the work. Since you've presented yourself as a problem solver, they'll like helping you.
- If you don't have a list of referrals from earlier contacts, you can call them back and ask them: "Is there anyone you can think of who I could talk to that could help me with this?" or "Do you know anyone who might know people I could contact for advice on this project?"
- Warm referrals tend to be easier than cold calls. If contacting someone new makes you nervous, try to find a mutual contact to introduce you.
- You don't have to know all ten valuable people before you contact your first.
- You can get new contacts from conversations in this exercise.

I have given this exercise to hundreds of students, and all have managed to finish, many with no experience cold calling before. You can too.

However challenging they expected it at first, they loved the experience after doing it.

Action

As one student found, "I've learned to be comfortable outside of my comfort zone. It was definitely scary to talk not only to people I don't know, but also to important people in the field. It was hard to draw the line between going through the motions and actually putting my plan into action in this exercise. But once I started making calls, it got easier and I started to understand the real goal of the project."

Here are your actions for this exercise:

1. List ten people with value to your project whom you can reach. (If you can't list ten yet, add the rest from referrals that come while doing this exercise.)
2. Schedule a meeting with each in turn. Use referrals if you can and introductory emails that worked before if you can't.
3. Tell each about the project so far and get five pieces of advice from each.
4. Close each conversation with the same two questions:
   i) "Is there anything to add that I didn't think to bring up?"
   ii) "Is there anyone you can think of I could talk to who could help me with this?"
5. If you believe the advice will improve your solution, implement it before presenting to the next person.
6. Continue until you've received advice from ten people.

As in earlier conversations, describe the ideas conversationally, without presentations or slides—a sentence or two if possible.

Lead the conversations to get advice, deflect judgment, and defer long digressions, as you did in earlier exercises.

Conversing by email doesn't count for this exercise. You can schedule by email, and converse by video or phone if necessary, but meet ideally in person.

Deliverables

One student shared his results from this exercise: "I was able to talk to some very valuable people in the field, including a Stanford professor who had a lot of startup companies in Silicon Valley, including one that was sold for $360 million. I also talked to the CEO of a startup device accessory company in New Jersey who gave me great feedback on my idea and wished to speak to me again. He was an entrepreneurship student at Lehigh University. He and his roommate are now fully devoted to growing their company. He referred me to an executive at a successful device accessory company. Overall I learned a lot about what it means to make business connections and how successful they can be."

The deliverables for this exercise are:

1. A list of **the advice you got.** If you want, you can name the people who advised you, by initial or first name if you want to keep them anonymous.
2. Written below that, an **improved version of the problem and solution** based on that advice.
3. Below that, a list of any **referrals** to people who could help (use initials if you want to keep them anonymous).
4. Below that, your **reflections** on the experience.

You could work from the same template you used in exercises 4 and 6:

Old Problem: Sometimes people get caught in the rain and the cheap temporary umbrellas they have break.

Old Solution: Vending machines in subway stations with higher quality umbrellas, but more affordable by saving labor costs.

Advice 1:

Advice 2:

[...]

Advice 30:

New Problem: Same as old problem.

New Solution: Vending machines in convenience stores, safer than subways.

New Contacts: [*list of people referred to*]

Tips

Most people appreciate being contacted as a knowledgeable source of advice. Students routinely find that most people they talk to in this exercise *thank them* for the interaction.

Try for referrals to create warm connections instead of cold calls. If someone referred you and agreed that you could use their name, use it as early as possible. I usually use it in the subject, something like "John Doe referral."

Mentioning conversations you've had from earlier exercises will generally warm people to you, especially when the person you're talking to knows the person from the past conversation.

If you introduce yourself by email, I recommend keeping it short while still including enough detail to interest them. I recommend against describing yourself and the project in depth and then asking them for advice in your first approach—this asks too much of their time and often results in short responses that close the connection. Instead, write something like:

Subject: Alex Smith referral

Hi Pat,

Alex Smith suggested contacting you. I'm working on a project for a class in entrepreneurship and I'm looking for advice to improve my project. I wonder if you'd be available for a call to answer a few short questions to give me advice.

Thank you,
[Your name]

Without a referral, I'd write:

Hi Pat,

I'm working on a project for a class in entrepreneurship and I'm looking for advice to improve my project. I came across your name as an expert in the field. I wonder if you'd be available for a call to answer a few short questions to give me advice.

Thank you,
[Your name]

Feel free to put it in your words while keeping the structure where it works.

If they judge your ideas instead of giving advice, I recommend patiently and politely responding with the technique you developed talking to friends, family, and people in the field. Likewise, you may feel motivated to express judgment about their advice too. Instead, practice saying "thank you" for advice you don't like or can't use. You don't have to act on any advice.

End each conversation with:

1. Is there anything to add that I didn't think to bring up?
2. Is there anyone you can think of I could talk to who could help me with this?

Keep trying to get as many referrals as you can.

Checklist

☐ Did you contact at least ten people?
☐ Did you close each conversation with the two final questions?

Post-exercise Reflection

Before continuing, reinforce what you learned by reflecting. Put distractions away and spend a few minutes thinking about what you learned.

You can reflect on what you like, but here are some questions you might consider:

• Is your understanding of this course's seven principles changing? If so, how?
• How did you feel about the exercise before starting it?
• How would you have felt about it before starting this course?
• How do you feel about connecting with valuable people in general?

- Did any conversations go poorly? Did you or your project suffer in the long term for it?
- Did anyone share problems with you that you could make into job offers?

The 7 Principles

1. Personality matters less than skills you can learn.
2. The idea of a lifetime comes once a month.
3. Better than a great idea is an okay idea plus market feedback, flexibility, and iterations.
4. Start where you are with what you have.
5. Pitch and they'll judge. Ask advice and they'll help.
6. The problem leads to the solution.
7. Almost nothing inspires like helping others so much that they reward you for it.

REVIEW

TO REFRESH YOUR memory of the exercises you did:
Unit 1: **You and a Problem You Care About**
- Set a baseline: **Personal Essay**
- Start focusing on the problem: **5 Unsolved Problems**
- Start involving others: **5 Close Contacts**

Unit 2: **Creating Community**
- Getting advice and building community: **10 Friends and Family Members**
- Understand the problem viscerally: **5 People Who Feel the Problem**
- Building community in your field: **10 People Closer to Your Field**

Unit 3: **Refining Your Solution**
- How your organization works: **Create a Visual Model**
- Learn details and show viability: **Details, Sustainability, and Financials**

Unit 4: **Creating Professional Relationships with Valuable People**
- Set your foundation as a valuable member of your field: **Second Personal Essay**
- Build high-value community, get job offers: **Valuable People**
- Reflect, review, and plan: **This Review**

You finished the exercises. Here's a new chance to reflect and look forward. If you're inclined to write more, here are some questions and topics to think about while writing:

- What are the three most valuable things you learned?
- What do you think about initiative and entrepreneurship now?
- What do you think about responsibility, identifying and solving problems, creating projects, creating relationships, and creating teams?
- What works for you in these areas? What doesn't?
- What are your models of taking initiative and entrepreneurship? Of someone who takes initiative? Of how initiative works?
- What motivated you to do these exercises?
- Where do you want to apply what you've learned?
- What are your memories of taking initiative? How do they relate to what you learned?
- Did you switch projects? If so, how did the new one compare with the old one?
- Did your level of passion change? If so, how?

Low-Level Details

If you've just read the book for the first time without launching a project, I want to remind you of the simplicity of starting. Repeating from what I said at the beginning of Part Two, I recommend one of three first steps.

Option one is to get out a piece of paper and pen or to open a document on your computer and start the first personal essay. This option has the advantage of being free and you can start immediately. Its downside is that it lacks the motivation and feedback of public accountability.

Option two is to create your essay on a blog service. This option is also free. You can make the blog anonymous or not, as you prefer. You can choose whom you tell about it.

Option three is to sign up for the online course at spodek
academy.com and start writing your essay on the forum there. This
option is not free, but the discount code INITIATIVEBOOK gives
a 25-percent discount. More importantly, the forum is populated
by people going through the same process as you, so you can ask,
share, and learn from each other's experiences. It also contains
videos of me describing the exercises, and emails you reminders
to stay on track.

Once you get out that paper or create that account, you'll find
continuing easier.

EPILOGUE

THE MEDIA AND ACADEMICS prognosticate that today's jobs won't exist tomorrow, trying to scare us into thinking we aren't prepared and can't prepare. They suggest that artificial intelligence and robots will make our jobs obsolete. They say we are becoming increasingly isolated.

You've read the articles. In a typical example, *The Guardian* states[1] that "experts now predict that a tipping point in robotic deployments is imminent—and that much of the developed world simply isn't prepared for such a radical transition... Somehow, we believe our livelihoods will be safe. They're not: every commercial sector will be affected by robotic automation in the next several years."

Method Initiative suggests otherwise.

These doomsayers base their views on an outdated view of work, jobs, and relationships. Sadly, they lead people to continue seeking income by sending résumés and hoping to find jobs instead of creating them. Looking for work that way says, "please pay me, I'll do anything you ask"—not particularly dignified, if you ask me, nor likely to lead to meaningful work.

If you don't create opportunities, what can you do but accept what the employer offers?

You don't have to accept that model. Here's another:

1. There's you.
2. There's what you need and want to live—food, water, shelter, money, furniture, appliances, internet connections, love, support, and so on.
3. Between you and these resources are people who control access to them.
4. If you behave and communicate in ways that motivate those people to reciprocate and reward you, they will.

Method Initiative teaches you to behave and communicate those ways.

Increased automation *improves* a Method Initiator's situation. You can choose what communities you want to work with by choosing what problems to solve. Less menial work means more social interaction, where Method skills shine. Automation enables you to base your projects on human connection.

No matter what fields are automated, a Method Initiator lacking resources can find people with them, identify their problems, help solve them, and receive access to the resources.

More technology improves a Method Initiator's situation too. Many people worry that tech jobs require training and become obsolete increasingly fast. But tech work requires leadership, management, and vision.

Tech people tend to work in solution space, putting technology before people. Method Initiators tend to work in the problem space. We work with *people* to solve their problems. When new technologies enable new solutions, we use them, so knowing how technologies work helps, but we can just as well involve tech workers in the process.

Since Method Initiators and tech workers work in complementary spaces, they don't compete. Method Initiators want *more* tech workers. We welcome their growth, not fear it. Tech workers become another circle in the visual model of exercises 7 and 8. Method Initiative skills bring meaning, value, and purpose to technology.

Method Initiative leads you to see people's problems as opportunities to help them so that they reward you. Helping people with greater resources usually means greater reward per person helped. Helping people with lesser resources usually means you help more people. Resources can be material, like food and money, or like connections to others or emotional support.

As I see it, Method Initiative helps society redistribute resources voluntarily and mutually beneficially. If you lack a resource others have, you can initiate ways to help them.

Initiators who see people as people first—not as labels or positions on an organization chart, as job seekers tend to—have always and will always find ways to help people enough that they reward us back. We enjoy the process because almost nothing inspires like helping others so much that they reward you for it.

That's why many successful initiators leave school before finishing. When you know you can help people enough that they'll reward you and you'll enjoy doing it, learning more facts, taking more tests, and writing more papers distract you from helping people. Anyone who likes academic learning can always take more classes, which they'll do out of desire, not coercion.

Method Living

The way Method Initiative brings people together at work to cooperate and collaborate on passions, not just transactions, it does so in the rest of life. It replaces isolation and alienation with support and understanding.

Living by Method principles, *Method Living*, makes life about people—empathy, compassion, service, action, listening, understanding, making others feel understood, and so on. Once you start Method Living, there's no going back.

Method Initiative and Education

I've taught Method Initiative to students as young as high school. They loved it, saying things like this anonymous student did: "During the beginning of this course I didn't really believe that I could be able to come up with a good idea that I might be able to take to market. I didn't know that so many good ideas just occurred to everyone so often, and that really gave me inspiration and resolve to just work on my idea even harder."

You saw how it led to them tackling challenging issues in the finance exercise. What people who haven't done Method Initiative expect to be hardest becomes the most engaging when acting on their initiative, not on others' out of coercion. Teens aren't too young nor is any age too old.

I've often said and still hold that if this course and my leadership course had been available I would have taken them instead of business school—and Columbia's was in the top five at the time. Business schools and their networks may be the best resource for people going into banking, consulting, or multinational corporate work, but for anything else, the ability to initiate a project and lead it creates a more fulfilling life of service, more security, and more meaningful relationships. Learning it takes a lot less time and resources.

I often describe Method Initiative and Method Leadership as the fastest, cheapest way to get an MBA: start a project, grow it, lead it to where you need the professional services of an MBA, and hire one. There's your MBA! The MBA you hire will likely appreciate your hiring them for likely having created more interesting work and creating more meaning, value, importance, purpose, and passion than most jobs.

Beyond people using this book to learn and practice Method Initiative for themselves, I hope teachers and parents use it to teach the next generation to look forward to change with confidence and enthusiasm. Other programs I've seen seem relatively contrived instead of based on what successful initiators do. They seem jargon-filled, less personal, and more aimed at transactions and entrepreneurship appreciation than relationships, meaning, purpose, and passion.

Students whose projects take off have told me they were considering leaving school to run them in the style of many successful initiators, and have asked me for advice. I suggest they get that advice from their parents, but whatever their choice, having the option improves their lives. If they stay, they will stay to enjoy school more, learn more, and participate in extracurriculars more. They'll learn because they want to, not out of fear or coercion.

Isn't that what we want for ourselves and our children—the ability, desire, and skills to serve others while enjoying life themselves, creating meaning, value, importance, purpose, and passion?

All it takes is practice.

NOTES

Preface

1. Ben Casselman, "A Start-Up Slump Is a Drag on the Economy. Big Business May Be to Blame," *New York Times*, Sep. 20, 2017, https://www.nytimes.com/2017/09/20/business/economy/startup-business.html
2. Eduardo Porter, "Where Are the Start-Ups? Loss of Dynamism Is Impeding Growth," *New York Times*, Feb. 6, 2018, https://www.nytimes.com/2018/02/06/business/economy/start-ups-growth.html

Chapter 1: The Problem

1. "STEM Jobs: 2017 Update," U.S. Department of Commerce, https://www.commerce.gov/news/reports/2017/03/stem-jobs-2017-update
2. Emily Canal, "We Fact-Checked Seven Seasons of *Shark Tank* Deals. Here Are the Results," *Forbes*, Oct. 21, 2016, https://www.forbes.com/sites/emilycanal/2016/10/21/about-72-of-deals-that-happen-on-shark-tank-dont-turn-out-as-seen-on-tv
3. Paul Graham, "The 18 Mistakes That Kill Startups," blog entry on paulgraham.com, Oct. 2006, http://paulgraham.com/startupmistakes.html
4. Drake Baer, "The Making of Tesla: Invention, Betrayal, and the Birth of the Roadster," *Business Insider*, Nov. 11, 2014, https://www.businessinsider.com/tesla-the-origin-story-2014-10
5. "Google Code of Conduct," as archived and accessed July 31, 2018, at https://web.archive.org/web/20190123053753/https://abc.xyz/investor/other/google-code-of-conduct.html

Chapter 2: The Dog Show and Culture

1. Eric Nagourney, "Checklist Reduces Deaths in Surgery," *New York Times*, Jan. 20, 2009, https://www.nytimes.com/2009/01/20/health/20surgery.html

2. Sebastian Rausch and Hagen Schwerin, "Does Higher Energy Efficiency Lower Economy-Wide Energy Use?" (working paper, Center of Economic Research at ETH Zurich, Oct. 2018), https://www.ethz.ch/content/dam/ethz/special-interest/mtec/cer-eth/cer-eth-dam/documents/working-papers/WP-18-299.pdf

Chapter 4: Our Misguided Educational System

1. Suniya Luthar and Aparna Sampat, "Executive Summary of Findings from the Community Youth Survey, Mercer Island," (working paper, Teachers College, Columbia University, Dec. 2006), https://www.mercergov.org/Files/CTC%20Executive%20Summary.doc
2. Joshua Spodek, "Watch and read *Most Likely to Succeed*," blog entry on joshuaspodek.com, Nov. 2, 2016, http://joshuaspodek.com/watch-read-succeed

Chapter 5: The Solution, Part 2: Method Initiative

1. Interview available at http://joshuaspodek.com/guests/col-everett-spain
2. Carrie Kerpen, "Three Important Lessons Women Learn Early in Their Careers," *Forbes*, Feb. 17, 2017, https://www.forbes.com/sites/carriekerpen/2017/02/14/three-important-lessons-women-learn-early-in-their-careers

Chapter 6: The Myths

1. TEDx talk available at http://joshuaspodek.com/rjs-tedx-talk-began-homework

Chapter 7: 3 Antidotes and 7 Principles

1. Paul Light, "Reshaping Social Entrepreneurship," *Stanford Social Innovation Review*, Fall 2006, http://www.nyu.edu/social-entrepreneurship/news_events_resources/pdf/paul_light.pdf

Chapter 8: Initiative, Action, and Passion

1. Seth Godin, *Footprints on the Moon* (New York: Do You Zoom, Inc., 2017).
2. Brian Bollinger and Kenneth Gillingham, "Peer Effects in the Diffusion of Solar Photovoltaic Panels," (paper, NYU Stern School of Business, Yale School of Forestry & Environmental Studies, 2012), http://environment.yale.edu/gillingham/BollingerGillingham_PeerEffectsSolar.pdf

Overview

1. Giada Di Stefano et al., "Learning by Thinking: How Reflection Aids Per-formance," (working paper, HEC Paris, Harvard University, University of North Carolina, 2014), http://www.sc.edu/uscconnect/doc/Learning%20 by%20Thinking,%20How%20Reflection%20Aids%20Performance.pdf

Exercise 2: 5 Unsolved Problems

1. Kerpen, "Three Important Lessons."

Epilogue

1. Dan Shewan, "Robots Will Destroy Our Jobs—and We're Not Ready for It," *The Guardian*, Jan. 11, 2017, https://www.theguardian.com/technology/2017/jan/11/robots-jobs-employees-artificial-intelligence

FEEDBACK

FEWER THAN 1 PERCENT of readers review books online, but nearly everyone relies on reviews. If you liked this book, please review it to help others find it. If you didn't like it, I welcome constructive criticism. You can reach me at joshuaspodek.com/contactconnect.

ABOUT THE AUTHOR

JOSHUA SPODEK is a TEDx speaker, professor at NYU, host of the award-winning *Leadership and the Environment* podcast, a columnist for *Inc.* magazine, and author of the #1 bestselling book *Leadership Step by Step*. He holds five Ivy League degrees, including a PhD in astrophysics and an MBA from Columbia, where he studied under a Nobel laureate and helped build an X-ray observational satellite with the European Space Agency and NASA.

Josh left academia to found a venture based on his invention that showed animated images to subway riders between stations. Today, he teaches and coaches leadership and entrepreneurship at NYU and at Columbia Business School, and has spoken at Harvard, Princeton, West Point, MIT, BCG, PwC, S&P, and IBM. He has appeared on every major network, and has been featured in the *New York Times*, the *Wall Street Journal*, and many other publications. In its "Genius" issue, *Esquire* listed him among the "best and brightest"; NBC has called him an "astrophysicist turned new media whiz," and *Forbes* and ABC have called him a "rocket scientist."

Josh has done burpees daily since 2011 (129,000 and counting at the time of writing this book), takes 16 months to produce one load of garbage, and hasn't flown (by choice) since March 2016. He blogs daily at joshuaspodek.com and makes his courses available online at spodekacademy.com.

Made in the USA
Columbia, SC
14 January 2022

54268801R00155